For Whose Pleasure?

*Confronting the Real Issue
as We Gather to Worship*

by

Steve Klingbeil

Publishing

Published by
Innovo Publishing, LLC
www.innovopublishing.com
1-888-546-2111

Publishing

Providing Full-Service Publishing Services for
Christian Authors, Artists & Organizations: Hardbacks, Paperbacks,
eBooks, Audiobooks, Music & Videos

FOR WHOSE PLEASURE?
Confronting the Real Issue as We Gather to Worship
Copyright © 2011 by Steve Klingbeil
All rights reserved.

Unless otherwise indicated, Scripture is taken from The Holy Bible, English Standard Version, copyright © 2001 by Crossway Bibles, a division of Good News Publishers, www.esvstudybible.org.

Scripture marked KJV is taken from the King James Version of the Bible.

Scripture marked NASB is taken from the New American Standard Bible®, Copyright © 1960, 1962, 1963, 1968, 1971, 1972, 1973, 1975, 1977, 1995 by The Lockman Foundation.

Scripture marked NIV is taken from the HOLY BIBLE, NEW INTERNATIONAL VERSION®. NIV®. Copyright © 1973, 1978, 1984 by International Bible Society.

Scripture marked NLT is taken from the Holy Bible, New Living Translation, copyright © 1996, Tyndale House Publishers, www.newlivingtranslation.com.

All italics within Scripture quotations have been added by the author.

ISBN 13: 978-1-936076-58-1
ISBN 10: 1-936076-58-6

Cover Design & Interior Layout: Innovo Publishing, LLC

Printed in the United States of America
U.S. Printing History

First Edition: January 2011

Contents

Acknowledgments

My love and thanks to Becky. Twenty-two great years and counting. She always believes in me. I am blessed.

And thanks to my kids, Caroline, Connor, and Callie, who have always been great sports when I have told stories about them in church—except for the time I let it slip that we have a bathroom in our house. It was something about seeking shelter in a storm, but they were mortified that the whole church found out that we have a bathroom. Scandalous! Sorry, guys.

Thanks to Liberty Bible Church for graciously and generously granting me a sabbatical leave to work on this project. And my appreciation to Lois Stück for her editing work.

Introduction

My three kids play soccer. They started as preschoolers, and in those days my wife, Becky, and I fondly called the game Amoeba-Ball. At that age the players haven't yet figured out how to play a position, so they all just cluster around the ball—following wherever it goes and resembling a giant amoeba. It's fun and very cute. Once in a while a little kid gets confused and starts kicking the ball in the wrong direction. The coaches yell, parents holler, but the little squirt is oblivious and kicks the ball into the wrong net. Nobody minds too much. The coach might look exasperated for a moment but soon remembers that the child is four years old. So the coach just reminds the kid which way to go next time. The child might look embarrassed for a moment but soon recovers. Parents smile and laugh, and it's no big deal. Aggressive play, good footwork for a preschooler, great shot . . . *wrong goal.*

We've seen it happen in basketball too. Our youngest daughter, Callie, has played a few seasons now, so the team's skills have greatly improved. But when her team first started, it was chaotic. The game can be confusing for a ten-year-old playing for the first time. It's hard to remember which way to go in the middle of jump-balls, possession arrows, fouls, out-of-bounds plays, turnovers, free-throws, offensive sets, defensive sets, and everything else. We have seen girls get confused and score for the other team. Strong move, great shot . . . *wrong basket.*

Putting the ball in the wrong goal may be cute for a four-year-old soccer player or a preteen basketball player, but not so much for a seasoned veteran. It happens accidentally sometimes, even at the World Cup level of soccer. They call it an "own goal." While attempting to clear the ball out of the box, a defender might inadvertently kick it the wrong way and into the net. I did that myself in a game in which the parents took on their kids. Very embarrassing. But I've never seen a mature player get so confused as to dribble the ball the wrong way and *purposefully* shoot against his or her own goalkeeper. It probably has happened, but it would be a strange experience for everyone watching and playing. How could you explain it?

That strange scenario—aiming at the wrong goal—can happen as Christians gather to worship. There is *right worship* and there is *wrong worship*. There is worship that is aimed at an entirely right goal and worship that is aimed at an entirely wrong goal. As the worshiping church has emerged from the last forty or more years of struggle and change, an outcome of the worship transformations is that our purposes in worshiping have become skewed. We've come out kicking at the wrong goal. Not that we had it right forty or fifty years ago. Back in 1961, A. W. Tozer preached what has since become a famous sermon, "Worship: the Missing Jewel of the Evangelical Church." In Tozer's words:

> The greatest tragedy in the world today is that God has made man in His image and made him to worship Him, made him to play the harp of worship before the face of God day and night, but he has failed God and dropped the harp. It lies voiceless at his feet. . . .
>
> We have almost everything, but there's one thing that the churches, even the gospel churches, do not have: that is the ability to worship. We are not cultivating the art of worship. It's the one shining gem that is lost to the modern church, and I believe that we ought to search for this until we find it.[1]

From Tozer's perspective, there was not even much of an effort to worship in 1961. Christians then weren't even trying to kick the ball, much less score a goal. We don't want to return to that. Much has changed and Tozer would do a double take if he visited our churches today. But the value of all the effort and energy invested in worship since the 1960s is questionable if it has been misguided. I am going to argue that even as we are witnessing unprecedented enthusiasm and passion in our worship endeavors, the church is being challenged as much as at any time in history by the seduction of wrong worship. We are aiming at the wrong goal. And it doesn't matter how impressively our church kicks the ball if it is kicking it in the wrong direction.

I'm not typically an in-your-face kind of guy, but this is a confrontational book. If you and I are engaged in wrong worship, we need to recognize it and be challenged to change. I sense that worshipers want to worship rightly; I certainly want to worship rightly. But even after all of the worship services, the sermons, the books, and the workshops, we may still have blinders on and not clearly see God's desires for our worship. We may not even understand that we are kicking the ball the wrong way. So I am confronting you, and myself, about our worship.

You may not buy it. Aiming at the right goal in worship will mean adopting new attitudes and behaviors. It will entail change. I am a worship pastor, and I hear the thoughts and feelings of worshipers at my church and elsewhere. I've been doing some classroom teaching recently, and I have also been teaching an online worship class for several years. I get to read many "worship service observations" and "worship leader interviews" from across the country and around the world, so I get a great sampling of comments from worshipers all over the place. I haven't collated the information into a scientific survey or study, but I do have a pretty good spot on the bleachers to observe and listen. From these observations, I know that many worshipers do not view worship as an area of personal growth. We often want to change the externals of worship, but we aren't as conscious of the need for internal adjustments. We don't *want* to change. But that's where the pursuit of right worship begins. This book is about making intentional and often hard choices, and that takes spiritual maturity and the willingness to change and grow.

Unfortunately, worshiping rightly will be difficult if we are spiritual babies. And the level of our spiritual maturity does not necessarily coincide with the number of years we have been a Christian. Paul wrote to the Corinthians:

> But I, brothers, could not address you as spiritual people, but as people of the flesh, as infants in Christ. I fed you with milk, not solid food, for you were not ready for it. And even now you are not yet ready, for you are still of the flesh. For *while there is jealousy and strife among you*, are you not of the flesh and behaving only in a human way?
>
> 1 Corinthians 3:1–3

The fact that the Corinthians were quarreling with each other told Paul that they still had some growing up to do. They were infants. This principle applies to our corporate worship: the worship wars are mostly over, but skirmishes continue. The fact that worship has been and still is a contentious issue shows that we have been spiritual babies. We have subsisted on milk in our thinking about worship and haven't yet developed a taste for solid food. To worship rightly, we need to grow. I hope the challenges in this book give us an opportunity to sample some solid food. Let's get off the milk already! If our worship is misguided, let's figure it out. If there is something wrong with the direction our worship is going, let's get it turned around. Let's look inside and be willing to mature in our worship. I am writing to myself as well as to you because I know my own heart, and if you are anything like me, you have room for growth as a worshiper.

The approach will be to learn from wrong worship in the Bible (chapter 1), recognize the wrong worship in today's worshiping church (chapter 2), and identify the right goal of worship (chapter 3). Then each of chapters 4 through 12 will address one of the nine biblical values in order to practically assist us in reaching that right goal.

Those nine values are:

1. gathering
2. authenticity
3. engagement
4. unity
5. truth
6. purity
7. sacrifice
8. fruit of our lips
9. action

Let's find God's truth, understand His desires, perceive what is the *real* issue in our worship, and become better worshipers.

1

Wrong Worship in Scripture

Let us offer to God acceptable worship, with reverence
and awe, for our God is a consuming fire.
Hebrews 12:28–29

Not every worship encounter in Scripture ends well.
Sometimes in life we can learn as much from bad examples
as we can from good examples. And unfortunately, there are
plenty of biblical examples of wrong worship to learn from.

Cain and Abel

It starts with Cain and Abel way back in Genesis 4.

Now Abel was a keeper of sheep, and Cain a
worker of the ground. In the course of time Cain
brought to the LORD an offering of the fruit of the
ground, and Abel also brought of the firstborn of his
flock and of their fat portions. *And the LORD had
regard for Abel and his offering, but for Cain and his
offering he had no regard.* So Cain was very angry,
and his face fell. The LORD said to Cain, "Why are
you angry, and why has your face fallen? If you do
well, will you not be accepted? And if you do not do
well, sin is crouching at the door. Its desire is for you,
but you must rule over it."

Genesis 4:2–7

Abel brought an offering that pleased God and was accepted. Cain brought an offering that was not pleasing to God and was not accepted. The text does not clearly explain why the offerings were regarded differently. It may have been that Abel's offering was more costly and showed greater devotion or that Abel brought the firstborn and Cain brought leftovers. Or there may have been a connection to the later Levitical system of sacrifices—a blood offering versus an offering of crops. We get a little more insight in the New Testament, where John says, "We should not be like Cain, who was of the evil one and murdered his brother. And why did he murder him? Because his own deeds were evil and his brother's righteous" (1 John 3:12). John asserts that Abel was righteous and Cain was not. The author of the book of Hebrews says, "By faith Abel offered to God a more acceptable sacrifice than Cain, through which he was commended as righteous, God commending him by accepting his gifts. And through his faith, though he died, he still speaks" (Heb. 11:4). We see that Abel was a man of faith, and we can infer that Cain was not. God's response to their sacrifices, therefore, was a response to who they were. It was a response to their view of God and their relationship with Him. It was a response to the condition of their hearts, their faith, and their righteousness, or in Cain's case, his lack of righteousness.

One thing from this episode is clear, and it is that worship can be wrong and unacceptable to God. Cain's worship had the wrong aim. If his heart wasn't in it, why did he present an offering at all? Perhaps he was competing with his brother. We see his murderous jealousy in the aftermath. Perhaps he was just going through the motions of fulfilling an obligation or an expectation, but his heart was not right and his worship did not please God.

Nadab and Abihu

Remember Nadab and Abihu? Here's the account from Leviticus 10:

> Now Nadab and Abihu, the sons of Aaron, each took his censer and put fire in it and laid incense on it and offered unauthorized fire before the LORD, which He had not commanded them. And fire came out from before the LORD and consumed them, and they died before the LORD. Then Moses said to Aaron, "This is what the LORD has said, 'Among those who are near me I will be sanctified, and before all the people I will be glorified.'" And Aaron held his peace.
>
> Leviticus 10:1–3

Worshiping is serious business. Worship can be wrong and can displease God. Nadab and Abihu were sons of Aaron—important guys. They climbed up Mount Sinai with Moses, Aaron, and seventy elders and saw God (Exod. 24:9–11). But something wasn't right in their attitudes, and they decided to worship their own way. They had their own ideas as to what worship should be like rather than aiming to please God by sacrificing His way. God showed His displeasure in a startling way that should motivate us to seriously reflect on our own worship.

King David and Uzzah

Equally sobering is the story of Uzzah. King David wanted to bring the ark of God from Kiriath-jearim to Jerusalem.

> And they carried the ark of God on a new cart, from the house of Abinab, and Uzzah and Ahio were driving the cart. And David and all Israel were rejoicing before God with all their might, with song and lyres and tambourines and cymbals and trumpets. And when they came to the threshing floor of Chidon,

3

Uzzah put out his hand to take hold of the ark, for the oxen stumbled. *And the anger of the LORD was kindled against Uzzah, and he struck him down because he put out his hand to the ark, and he died there before God.*

1 Chronicles 13:7–10

What made God so angry? In His earlier instructions regarding the tabernacle, He had given detailed rules for handling the articles of worship. This was one way in which God demonstrated His divine holiness and established the level of reverence with which worship was to be conducted. He prescribed a specific way for the ark to be transported: on poles and carried by Levites (Exod. 25:12–15; Num. 4:1–20). In addition, only certain Levites were allowed to handle the most holy items of the tabernacle. Others were not even allowed to "look on the holy things," much less touch them, "lest they die" (Num. 4:20).

God's punishment of Uzzah seems too severe when we read the passage to mean that he was simply trying to keep the ark from falling. David apparently thought so too. The following verses say that "David was angry because the LORD had broken out against Uzzah. And that place is called Perez-uzza to this day. And David was afraid of God that day, and he said, 'How can I bring the ark of God home to me?'" (1 Chron. 13:11–12). Once again the story shows that worship is not something to be taken lightly or casually, even in the handling of the ark. Although it was in the midst of a wonderful celebration in which "David and all Israel were rejoicing before God with all their might" (v. 8), David's apparent disregard for the mode of conveyance and Uzzah's touching the ark was wrong worship. It was displeasing to God. David and Uzzah were putting convenience or laziness or carelessness in front of their commitment to please God by worshiping *His* way.

David figured it out, and three months later he tried again (1 Chron. 13:14). This time, however, David declared that "no one but the Levites may carry the ark of God, for the LORD had chosen them to carry the ark of the LORD and to minister to him forever" (1 Chron. 15:2). Then he told the Levites:

> "Because you did not carry it the first time, the LORD our God broke out against us, because we did not seek him according to the rule." So the priests and the Levites consecrated themselves to bring up the ark of the LORD, the God of Israel. And the Levites carried the ark of God on their shoulders with the poles, as Moses had commanded according to the word of the LORD.
>
> 1 Chronicles 15:13–15

What followed was a glorious celebration as "all Israel" brought up the ark of the covenant of the Lord to the city of David. Unfortunately, David's wife Michal had issues with David's conduct, but that's another story.

Samuel and Saul

Accounts of God's anger and the consequences of wrong worship are hard stories to read. Another one occurs in 1 Samuel 13:

> Saul was still at Gilgal, and all the people followed him trembling. He waited seven days, the time appointed by Samuel. But Samuel did not come to Gilgal, and the people were scattering from him. So Saul said, "Bring the burnt offering here to me, and the peace offerings." And he offered the burnt offering. As soon as he had finished offering the burnt offering, behold, Samuel came. And Saul went out to meet him and greet him. Samuel said, "What have you done?" And Saul said, "When I saw that the people were scattering from me, and that you did not come within the days appointed, and that the Philistines had mustered at Michmash, I said, 'Now the Philistines will come down against me at Gilgal, and I have not sought the favor of the LORD.' So I forced myself, and

> offered the burnt offering." And Samuel said to Saul, *"You have done foolishly. You have not kept the command of the LORD your God, with which he commanded you.* For then the LORD would have established your kingdom over Israel forever. But now your kingdom shall not continue.
>
> 1 Samuel 13:7 14

Which commandment of God did Saul violate? It's hard to say for sure. He didn't wait long enough, or he wasn't sanctioned to perform the ceremony (Num. 18:7), or there is more to the story that we don't know. But it's clear that he was disobedient. Saul's aim was to deal with a bad situation that was getting worse, and to handle it himself. Panic. Lack of trust. Insecurity. Peer pressure. After all, the people were scattering. His aim was to keep control of the situation, but he tried to do it his own way. Rather than pleasing God by worshiping in obedience and waiting on God (and Samuel), his disobedience led to wrong worship and the end of his kingdom—another severe consequence for not worshiping God's way.

The Nation of Israel

On a broader scale, think about the long, often sordid, worshiping history of the Old Testament nation of Israel. Moses had some clear words for the people of God before he died in the land of Moab. The final chapters of Deuteronomy contain Moses's final sermons to the people as they were poised on the edge of the Promised Land, and he didn't mince words concerning the choice they had to worship rightly or worship wrongly. In chapter 30 he set the choice before them: life or death, good or evil, blessings or curses, right worship or wrong worship.

> See, I have set before you today life and good, death and evil. If you obey the commandments of the

LORD your God that I command you today, by loving
the LORD your God, by walking in his ways, and by
keeping his commandments and his statutes and his
rules, then you shall live and multiply, and the LORD
your God will bless you in the land that you are
entering to take possession of it. But if your heart turns
away, and you will not hear, but are drawn away to
worship other gods and serve them, I declare to you
today, that you shall surely perish. You shall not live
long in the land that you are going over the Jordan to
enter and possess. I call heaven and earth to witness
against you today, that I have set before you life and
death, blessing and curse. Therefore choose life, that
you and your offspring may live, loving the LORD
your God, obeying his voice and holding fast to him.
Deuteronomy 30:15–20

In presenting the choice, Moses provided a big carrot
and a big stick. Deuteronomy 28:1–14 contains a wonderful
litany of blessings if the people follow, obey, and worship God
alone. It is a beautiful passage of God's promised goodness and
love. God said that if the people faithfully obey His voice, they
will be blessed "in the city" and "in the field" (v. 3). He will
bless the "fruit of your womb and the fruit of your ground and
the fruit of your cattle," as well as "your basket and your
kneading bowl" (vv. 4–5). He will bless them in battle, causing
their enemies to "flee before you seven ways" (v. 7).

The LORD will open to you his good treasury,
the heavens, to give the rain to your land in its season
and to bless all the work of your hands. And you shall
lend to many nations, but you shall not borrow. And
the LORD will make you the head and not the tail, and
you shall only go up and not down, if you obey the
commandments of the LORD your God, which I
command you today (vv. 12–14).

How great is all of that? All of those blessings were
promised if the people would worship God alone. Conversely,

7

the remainder of chapter 28 contains a list of terrible curses that will follow disobedience and wrong worship:

> But if you will not obey the voice of the LORD your God or be careful to do all his commandments and his statutes that I command you today, then all these curses shall come upon you and overtake you. Cursed shall you be in the city, and cursed shall you be in the field. Cursed shall be your basket and your kneading bowl. Cursed shall be the fruit of your womb and the fruit of your ground, the increase of your herds and the young of your flock. Cursed shall you be when you come in, and cursed shall you be when you go out.
>
> The LORD will send on you curses, confusion, and frustration in all that you undertake to do, until you are destroyed and perish quickly on account of the evil of your deeds, because you have forsaken me. The LORD will make the pestilence stick to you until he has consumed you off the land that you are entering to take possession of it. The LORD will strike you with wasting disease and with fever, inflammation and fiery heat, and with drought and with blight and with mildew. They shall pursue you until you perish. And the heavens over your head shall be bronze, and the earth under you shall be iron. The LORD will make the rain of your land powder. From heaven dust shall come down on you until you are destroyed.
>
> Deuteronomy 28:15–24

That's only the first ten verses of curses; there are yet another forty-five. Really bad stuff.

For the Israelites, wrong worship usually started when they chose to comingle and intermarry with foreign nations and then got sucked into worshiping their idols. Right worship, on the other hand, was well defined: obedience and devotion to God and God alone as expressed through adherence to the Law and the sacrificial system. They were told to "love the LORD your God with all your heart and with all your soul and with all your might" (Deut. 6:5). If they loved God and obeyed Him, God would be pleased—which is the goal of worshiping rightly.

It is painful to continue reading the history of God's people throughout the Old Testament. They hung in there, mostly, as Joshua led them in their conquests. In his final days he reiterated their choice, exhorting them to "choose this day whom you will serve" (Joshua 24:15). But following Joshua's death, it didn't take long for the people to choose wrongly.

> And the people of Israel did what was evil in the sight of the LORD and served the Baals. And they abandoned the LORD, the God of their fathers, who had brought them out of the land of Egypt. They went after other gods, from among the gods of the peoples who were around them, and bowed down to them. And they provoked the LORD to anger.
>
> Judges 2:11–12

And so it began—cycles of sin and renewal. Over and over again, through the long histories of judges and kings, the people turned against God and sacrificed to the idols of foreign nations "on every high hill and under every green tree" (a phrase from 1 Kings 14:23, but repeated many times). God continually answered His people when they became overwhelmed by the consequences of their sin and called to Him in distress. But then they always succumbed to the worship of foreign gods and turned their backs on the one true God. I wince if a soccer player goes the wrong way on a soccer field, but that is insignificant compared to the feeling of painful anticipation as I read the stories of the delivering judges and the reforming kings knowing that in just a few verses the wrong worship will return and the people will disappoint God. It is a heart-breaking history. In every instance, they turned from pleasing God to worshiping sticks and stones. Jeremiah summed it up:

> This is what the LORD of Heaven's Armies,
> the God of Israel, says: "Take your burnt offerings and

your other sacrifices and eat them yourselves! When I led your ancestors out of Egypt, it was not burnt offerings and sacrifices I wanted from them. This is what I told them: 'Obey me, and I will be your God, and you will be my people. Do everything as I say, and all will be well!' But my people would not listen to me. They kept doing whatever they wanted, following the stubborn desires of their evil hearts. *They went backward instead of forward.*"

Jeremiah 7:21–24, NLT

Why did the Israelites choose wrong worship over and over and over again? Why does anyone worship any idol, even today? It is baffling and shocking. "'Has any nation ever traded its gods for new ones, even though they are not gods at all? Yet my people have exchanged their glorious God for worthless idols! The heavens are shocked at such a thing and shrink back in horror and dismay,' says the Lord" (Jer. 2:11–12, NLT).

We can only speculate that the Israelites chased after a more immediate sensory gratification in idol worship. They could see and touch idols. Worshiping the true God requires faith—"for we walk by faith, not by sight" (2 Cor. 5:7). They were seduced by the promise of sensual fulfillment. Partially, perhaps, their aim was to call their own shots, to make their own decisions, in essence, to rebel against the will and the Word of God. They aimed to please themselves rather than to please their God and Deliverer. And the consequences, of course, were devastating as God gave them over to the Babylonians and Assyrians and the nation of Israel experienced the diminution of David's kingdom.

The Pharisees

We have New Testament examples of wrong worship as well. In Mark 7 we read of some Pharisees and teachers of religious law confronting Jesus about eating with unwashed hands. I like the force of the New Living Translation in relating Jesus's comments:

> You hypocrites! Isaiah was right when he prophesied about you, for he wrote, "These people honor me with their lips, but their hearts are far from me. *Their worship is a farce*, for they teach man-made ideas as commands from God." For you ignore God's law and substitute your own tradition.
>
> Mark 7:6–8, NLT

Did you hear that? According to Jesus, their worship was a *farce*. That's a powerful indictment of wrong worship. The aim of the Pharisees was to look good by adhering to their own traditions rather than having an authentic relationship with the almighty God. They substituted God's ideas for worship with their own ideas.

Improper Communion

First Corinthians 11 contains some teaching regarding wrong worship as well:

> Whoever, therefore, eats the bread or drinks the cup of the Lord in an unworthy manner will be guilty concerning the body and blood of the Lord. Let a person examine himself, then, and so eat of the bread and drink of the cup. For anyone who eats and drinks without discerning the body eats and drinks judgment on himself. That is why many of you are weak and ill, and some have died.
>
> 1 Corinthians 11:27–30

Some of the Corinthians had a self-centered disregard for others in the body. A little bit earlier in the passage we see that "in eating, each one goes ahead with his own meal. One goes hungry, another gets drunk" (1 Cor. 11:21). In participating in the Lord's Supper, they were only aiming to please themselves rather than looking out for others. Wrong worship. And in this case, again, there were consequences: many got sick and some died.

Summary

It's possible to come to worship and kick at the wrong goal—to go backward instead of forward, as Jeremiah said. A couple thousand years have passed since the final words of God's Holy Word were penned. Today we don't bow before Baal idols or Ashtaroth poles. We aren't handling the ark, and we aren't faced with complying with every detailed instruction in Leviticus for sacrificing rightly. But every word in the Bible is true, and each one of these stories has relevance to the way we live and worship. We need to adjust our thinking to understand what constitutes wrong worship in our culture and recognize that it exists in our churches today. And we need to acknowledge that we are tempted to worship idols now every bit as much as the Israelites were so long ago.

Hebrews 12:28–29 calls us to "offer to God acceptable worship, with reverence and awe, for our God is a consuming fire." The "consuming fire" part should catch the attention of any who might offer *unacceptable* worship. Certainly in the past God responded with consuming fire when worship was unacceptable—remember Nadab and Abihu, Uzzah, and the Corinthians who died. Could He respond similarly today? Could He zap us if we aim the wrong way in our worship? Of course He could. Evidently He chooses not to—He works in different ways in different times—but He certainly *could*. But even if He doesn't punish us, God *feels the same way* about wrong worship now as He did in these stories. If He was angrily displeased with the wrong motives of Cain, Nadab and Abihu, Uzzah, Saul, the Israelites, the Pharisees, and the Corinthians, why wouldn't He be angrily displeased with wrong motives in our worship? God doesn't change. It should be a little scary for us to think that our worship might make God angry.

12

We have the same choice regarding our worship that Moses gave to the Israelites in Deuteronomy. Worship can be aimed at a wrong goal and be unacceptable to God, or worship can be aimed at the right goal, which is that of pleasing Him in every way.

Questions to Think About

1. What could *wrong worship* be like in your church?
2. Was the worship at church last Sunday *wrong* worship or *right* worship? Why?
3. Should we be more conscious that our worship can result in God's anger? Should we be more conscious that our worship can result in God's pleasure and blessing? Should this change anything in your worship?

2

The Wrong Goal in Today's Worshiping Church

For they all seek their own interests,
not those of Jesus Christ.
Philippians 2:21

How was church this last Sunday morning, Saturday evening, or whenever your church meets? Every church is different, so I'm sure that your experience was different than mine, but it is likely that you gathered with like-minded believers at a central location for growth, encouragement, worship, and possibly evangelism. It's likely that you entered a worship space together and experienced a sequence of events that included songs, prayer, the preaching of God's Word, and many other elements. It's likely that after the service you had the opportunity to fellowship with others in your church family. The details in different churches vary, maybe dramatically, but followers of Christ around the globe gather regularly, in whatever form they choose, to worship together.

Do you mind taking a little survey about the worship at your church? I'll tell you right up front that this is a *trick* survey—like a trick question. There are no right answers. And it's a trap. Once you've answered the questions I'm going to do my best to rip the whole thing to shreds. So I'm not sure what is in it for you—but do it anyway!

A Worship Survey

Answer each question on a scale from 1 to 10.
1 = not at all; 10 = very much

1. Some churches are *contemporary*, with praise teams, drums, guitars, synthesizers, and congas. Some are *traditional*, with piano, electric organ, and hymnals. Some are *liturgical*, with pipe organ and handbells. _____ Some are *blended*, with a combination of styles. Some have everything, with orchestras and more. Do you like the style at your church?

2. Is worship too loud? Too soft? Too much drum noise? Too much bass? Too much brass? Too much everything? Not enough choir? Do they forget to turn on the speakers? Are there always microphone _____ problems? Are you happy with the sound system and the volume in your worship in general?

3.   Some churches worship in cathedrals with stained glass, vaulted ceilings, statues of saints, and elaborate furnishings. Some worship in church buildings with pews, a pulpit, a choir loft, and a baptistery. Some meet in new, state-of-the-art worship facilities. Some worship in converted warehouses with pipes on the ceiling painted black or in schools or storefronts. Do you like your worship space?

4.   Are the songs you sing too shallow, too subjective, or too personal? Are the songs outdated, irrelevant, or just plain boring? Do you sing too many songs you don't know? Do you keep singing the same songs over and over? Do you never sing your favorite songs? How well do you like the songs you sing in worship?

5.   Does worship make you feel excited? Inspired? Motivated? Bored? Depressed? Impressed? Frustrated? Angry? Comfortable? Entertained? Stimulated? Uplifted? Do you like the way the worship at your church makes you feel?

6. Is there enough Scripture reading for you? Is there enough corporate prayer for you? Is it your opinion that the service should close with a benediction? Do you like creeds, responsive readings, times of confession? Do you like the multimedia presentations, drama, puppets, dance? Do you like it that they take an offering? Is there enough preaching? Too much preaching? Do you like the elements in your service? ———

7. Are the leaders boring? Are they too hyper? Do they dress right? Do they call attention to themselves? Are they condescending? Are they great communicators? Bad communicators? Great leaders? Bad leaders? Are they lay leaders? Are there people on the platform who annoy you? Distract you? Irritate you? Do enough people get to help lead? Are there people leading who shouldn't be leading? Do you like the leadership in your services? ———

8. Is the service impressive and professional? Is the band great? Is there a big megachurch WOW factor? Lights? Smoke? Cool platform sets? Cool visuals everywhere? Very slick? Or is it a simple setting? Plain? Nothing fancy, nothing new? No effort at all in the presentation? Does your church really need to get with it? Do you like the production level in your church worship service? ———

9. Is it easy or difficult to sing along? Are the songs in bad keys? Are there participatory elements such as creeds, prayers, responses? Do you know them? Do you have to stand when you would rather sit or sit when you would rather stand? Does it feel too dark to participate? Is it too bright and intimidating? Do you feel conspicuous? Do you feel lost? Do you like participating in the worship service?

10. Are those around you excited and enthusiastic enough? Is their worship joyful enough? Are they solemn and serious enough? Are they reverent enough? How do you like all of the chatting before the service? How about the clapping? Hand-raising? Dancing? Bowing? Tongues? Are you embarrassed, annoyed, or distracted by them? Do you like the behavior of the worshipers around you?

11. Are the pews too hard? Is it too hot in the room? Too cold? Are you physically comfortable?

12. Did we get everything? Is there anything else you like or don't like? The carpet? The number of announcements? Crying babies? Cell phones ringing? Style of communion cup? Are you happy with every other detail of the worship service?

Now add all the numbers in the right column, and if your total is. . . . Never mind. No need for more sarcasm.

Wrong Criteria for Evaluating Worship

This survey is a bit of a parody, but not much. It illustrates that people think about corporate worship in terms of *me*. All of the questions on the survey were about *me*. Ask anyone walking out of church, "How was the worship?" and the answer will most likely revolve around *me*—what *I* like, what *I* prefer, whether *I* was impressed, or how *I* felt. Ask that question, and the person most likely will really answer the question: "Was *I* pleased in worship?" Maybe there were a couple valid questions tucked in the survey—maybe—but we should recognize that we perceive worship through the lenses of our likes, our preferences, and ultimately our pleasure.

Here is a key truth: *Nowhere in Scripture is there any mention that a worshiper should be gratified in worship.* The worshiper is never the aim of biblical worship. The worshiper's likes, dislikes, feelings, and preferences are never factors in any worship encounter with the almighty God. It's not there. It's a little nervy of us, in fact, to think that we should humbly come into the presence of the Creator of the universe expecting to find personal pleasure. That's presumptive—maybe arrogantly so. Worship isn't about us. Worship isn't meant to please us. There is no biblical reason whatsoever that worship should be comfortable, non-threatening, enjoyable, impressive, entertaining, stimulating, uplifting, or anything else that we fancy. Biblical worship is often just the opposite: uncomfortable, threatening, and humbling. But if we think worship should be like that, or if we expect it, we are aiming at the wrong goal in our worship—the goal of pleasing self. This aim is manifest every time you or I talk about worship using the phrases "I like . . ," "I prefer . . . ," "I wish . . . ," "I need . . . ," "I think . . . ," or any other similar sentiment.

20

Causes of Self-Centered Worship

Why do we approach worship this way? It's because we are self-centered. That is not a new phenomenon. We have mentioned Nadab and Abihu. They wanted to worship the way they wanted to worship. Paul says of his fellow believers, "They all seek their own interests, not those of Jesus Christ" (Phil. 2:21). We all struggle with our sin nature and our love of self. Self-centeredness is evident practically from our birth. Ask any parent. It's only by the power of the Holy Spirit that any of us can become less self-centered and more selfless. And it's only going to get worse. Paul tells Timothy to understand that "in the last days there will come times of difficulty. For people will be *lovers of self*" (2 Tim. 3:1–5). So we shouldn't be surprised that we battle the idol of self in our worship. But there is much more to it, especially in contemporary society. Today's worshipers face enormous pressures to please self.

Societal Influences

I've become familiar with a book, written by secular authors Dr. Jean Twenge and Dr. Keith Campbell, entitled *The Narcissism Epidemic*. They write primarily about the United States, though the trends they observe have become global. The book chronicles the shifts in our culture toward blatant self-centeredness. They trace those shifts, beginning with the founding of America, the writing of our Constitution, and the principles of individual freedom tempered with equality. Twenge and Campbell say that in addition to freedom and equality, Americans have also historically adhered to the values of hard work and self-reliance. They make the case that these were all positive, political and social values throughout most of the history of the United States. Beginning in the 1960s, though, they notice change. As they put it, "The American flag of self-admiration slowly began to unfurl in the 1960s." For the next ten pages they document a transition from being a nation with a healthy sense of "individual liberty, freedom from tyranny, and fundamental equality," to becoming a culture that now espouses the ugly values of self-indulgence and self-absorption."

In the introduction to their book, the authors provide four "legs" upon which narcissism is built:

> Imagine narcissism in society resting on a four-legged stool. One leg is developmental, including permissive parenting and self-esteem-focused education. The second leg is the media culture of shallow celebrity. The third is the Internet: Despite its many benefits, the Web also serves as a conduit for individual narcissism. Finally, easy credit makes narcissistic dreams into reality.[3]

That was written before the credit bubble popped, but I doubt that our nation's recent economic woes have slowed the narcissism epidemic much. Twenge and Campbell examine these causes in depth and then go on to look at the *symptoms* of narcissism: vanity, materialism, uniqueness, antisocial behavior, relationship troubles, and entitlement. They then provide a chapter on religion and volunteering. It's a fascinating read. The book shows that we are living in an era that is unprecedented in its absorption with *me*. We are immersed in a culture that tells us every day and in myriads of ways that the primary value in life is to gratify self.

Christian Cultural Influences

And it's not as though the church has done much to combat this. We've mostly just gone along for the ride, so it is common to expect the church to cater to our self-gratification as well. In fact, in addition to the causes of self-absorption enumerated in Twenge and Campbell's "four-legged stool," I would add two other influences specifically within our Christian worship culture that have contributed even more to our self-centered focus: the Christian concert phenomenon and the seeker-oriented church growth model.

Christian Concerts

Over the last fifty years the contemporary Christian music scene has greatly influenced the worship in our churches. Do not misunderstand me as I explain this. I am *not* criticizing Christian recording artists—not their art, not their hearts, and not their intent. I use their music in worship, my kids listen to their recordings, and I've gone to their concerts. There are great Christian artists writing great songs that are impacting lives and strengthening faith. May God continue to bless their ministries. For the purposes of this study, however, please consider with me the unintended consequences of how Christian concert events and Christian recordings have blurred the distinction between worship and entertainment—between a worship gathering and a concert.

Christian artists are in the business of creating crowd appeal and pleasing the audience in order to sell tickets, CDs, and downloads. Of course they are; it's perfectly normal. The entertainment world is built on this premise: please the audience, and fame and fortune will follow. Every artist would love a packed house, and they pack the house by being hugely popular, and they become hugely popular by *pleasing their audience*. That's how it works. A Christian concert may very well be a wonderful worship experience—I believe that many are—but they are still fundamentally performance events designed to entertain and gratify the audience.

So as our worship venues look and sound more and more like our concert venues—which is what they are doing—the values and expectations spill over. Worshipers today are not able to distinguish between worship and performance; between a selfless worship experience and a self-gratifying entertainment experience. They expect to be equally pleased in both environments and expect worship leaders to deliver the

23

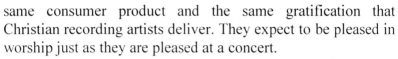

same consumer product and the same gratification that Christian recording artists deliver. They expect to be pleased in worship just as they are pleased at a concert.

Every two years the students at my church go to a humungous national youth conference. The conference organizers bring in top-notch Christian artists to lead the worship times, and most of the kids have a tremendous, mountaintop worship experience. They genuinely meet God, and life-changing decisions are made in that context. My oldest daughter's desire to serve as a missionary stems from one of these events. Great. I love it. But when the kids come back to worship on Sunday morning at church, our band isn't nearly as cool (they are cool, but not that cool), the music isn't as loud, we don't do smoke, and there aren't thousands of passionate young people on their feet waving glowsticks. Ninety-nine percent of churches in America can't replicate that kind of experience, and even if they could, they probably couldn't keep it fresh every Sunday. So the kids are bummed. Why doesn't our worship at church feel like the worship at the conference?

I'm going to get ahead of myself here, but this is where the rubber starts meeting the road in terms of becoming more mature worshipers. No matter how good the band is, we need to understand that our worship doesn't hinge on that kind of external stimulation. It hinges on the heart we bring and the choices we make. And neither does our worship hinge on how excited we get. God is very pleased with thousands of excited kids waving glowsticks and praising Him, but He is equally pleased with a broken, weary, hurting heart who comes in quietness to offer praise, love, and trust.

I'm not anti-concert, but I want my kids to dig down a layer or two deeper so they are able to personally meet and interact with God in just about any worshiping context: Exciting or not. On the mountaintop or in the valley. With their peeps or with their grandma. In a megachurch or in a struggling church of thirty. In Cairo, Chicago, Rio, or an Amazon jungle.

24

I have no issue with worship concerts—more power to 'em—but the real test of our worship maturity will often happen Sunday morning in our home church.

But I've gotten off topic. More of that later. We were talking about influences within our Christian culture that have made our worship more self-serving.

The Seeker-Oriented Church Growth Model

Way back when Willow Creek started developing its model, the premise of seeker-sensitivity was to create an environment that was non-churchy and non-threatening for those who were estranged from traditional church. The point was to give church a new feel that was comfortable and relevant so that the unchurched would come. These models have, of course, been dissected and analyzed every which way, and I think that Willow Creek has done a good bit of introspection themselves attempting to understand how effective the model has been.

The pendulum has done some swinging on this, and I won't try to opine on the evangelism or discipleship aspects of seeker-sensitivity. But I will say that this model has had far-reaching tentacles into the worship patterns of churches around the globe. Evangelical churches today, regardless of whether they overtly embrace seeker-sensitivity, are intent on designing *consumer-friendly* corporate worship in large part because of this growth model. Worshipers, of course, are attracted to the high production values, the hilarious skits, the awesome bands, and the clear teaching of Willow Creek type worship services. What's not to like? But of course that's the point. The worship is designed explicitly for the worshiper; it's a consumer model. So what does that teach worshipers? It teaches them to go to worship with the expectation of being entertained, tickled, and pleased. A more recent church growth model involves the formation of "video-venues." Churches offer a plethora of worship style choices in different rooms or sites, with the preaching projected on a screen. Again, what does that teach the worshipers? It teaches them to go to worship with the expectation of being entertained, tickled, and pleased—the wrong aim of worship.

Summary

So here's what we have: Our inherent sin nature and selfish desires are really enough of an issue right there to explain self-centered, wrong worship. We could have stopped with that. But we will keep going. Those of us who live in America and perhaps other Western cultures also have ingrained societal values regarding our individual rights and freedoms. This understanding of our societal rights can certainly be misunderstood in the context of church and lead us to think that we have a right to get what we want in worship. We expect this in so many other aspects of life (e.g., at Taco Bell, the shoe store, the car dealer) that it feels perfectly natural at church.

Going further, according to Twenge and Campbell's book, *The Narcissism Epidemic*, since the 1960s we have been influenced by: (1) permissive parenting and self-esteem-focused education, (2) the media culture of shallow celebrity, (3) the Internet, and (4) easy credit. Their book explores these causes more fully, but their ultimate argument is that Western society has become thoroughly and awfully self-absorbed. The authors also talk about advertising, and we could list a zillion ads on TV that further illustrate our obsessions with having everything "my way." Virtually every marketing technique on air and in print hones in on our self-indulgent proclivities.

I've tacked onto the list a couple uniquely Christian phenomena that in many ways parallel these other societal factors, namely: (1) the Christian concert scene and (2) the seeker-sensitive and video-venue church growth models. And I'm sure there are many other influencers that could be added to this list.

26

We live in a time and a culture that has exerted enormous influences on the way we think about life in general, but also on our approach to worship. It might seem inexplicable if a seasoned soccer player turned around, dribbled the wrong way, and shot against his own goalkeeper, but that's exactly what we are doing in our worship. Our thinking is twisted, and we are aiming at the wrong goal. We go backward rather than forward as we aim to *please ourselves*. The right biblical goal that I hope will become increasingly clear as we continue is *to please God*.

Our self-focused thinking is deeply ingrained. When we talked about it in my class, the students were quick to agree that we should worship to please God and not ourselves. Yet the very next week in class the students were back to talking about the styles they prefer, the kind of worship they like, and format with which they are most comfortable. It's hard for us to think differently, and we often don't even see it. Or when we see it, the pressures and habits are too strong for us to actually change and function differently. It will take tremendous effort to reverse our attitudes and our behaviors.

Back to Twenge and Campbell for a moment. What really caught my attention in their book is a segment in which one of the authors tells of a visit to a church. This was his experience:

> Keith was raised in the Episcopal church. He went to traditional services (yes, a little boring), showed up because he felt compelled, and had absolutely no narcissistic needs met by the church. . . . Recently, however, Keith had a very different religious experience—one that would have kept him attending church had he discovered it when he was younger. He went to a Southern California megachurch with his sister's family. Filled with options, the church was a giant, customizable religious emporium. Coffee stands (with high-end coffee, not the cheap stuff) were open throughout the expansive church grounds. You could

watch the service from inside the stadium, from just outside, or in a coffee shop/bookstore on a flat-screen TV (an option Keith's sister called "church-lite"). The service itself started with a set by a talented and inspiring musician who sounded like Dave Matthews. The words to the music were projected on a screen, so you could sing along if you wanted (this was a choice, too). A motivational speaker followed, telling a fantastic story with a personal life message (with a reference to Paul from the Bible). After the service ended everyone had donuts—and more really good coffee—while the kids played on the lawn. Keith was happy, the kids were happy (there'd been video games and live music in the Sunday school building), and it was a beautiful Southern California day.

In one sense, the service demanded nothing. It was really entertaining. There was a huge degree of personal choice, and no kneeling—unless you wanted to. By adapting to today's self-oriented culture, this megachurch was able to bring people back to religion. Many of those who joined would start thinking about God more, some would study the Bible in detail, some would become better and more caring citizens, some would volunteer to help the world, and some would ultimately become less narcissistic. This odd bit of alchemy—taking narcissism and trying to turn it into altruism—is at the heart of much modern religion.[4]

That's kind of a mixed review. The authors do recognize the potential for spiritual growth at this church. But it is amazing to me what two *secular* authors observed at this church: "*Filled with options, the church was a giant, customizable religious emporium.*" Wow. Worshiping with the aim of pleasing self is the wrong worship in today's church. It is aiming at the wrong goal. The Israelites turned to Baal and Ashtaroth; we turn to self.

Remember the survey at the beginning of the chapter? That kind of thinking has to go; it is self-centered worship.

That is worship aimed at pleasing ourselves. How do we even begin to think differently and approach worship differently? It's not enough to just recognize that we are self-centered and want to change. The pressures are too pervasive. We can't just eliminate self-absorption and create a vacuum. As is often true when we want to change wrong thinking or wrong behaviors, we need to *replace* the wrong thinking with something else— we need to replace it with right thinking. We need to locate the *right* goal and put our energies into that pursuit. Only then will we worship rightly.

Questions to Think About

1. Do you expect to be pleased or gratified in corporate worship? If so, where did your attitude come from?
2. Is worship at your church generally driven by a consumer mentality of pleasing the worshiper?
3. What would change if you came to worship without expecting self-gratification?

3

The Right Goal of Worship

Let the words of my mouth and the meditation
of my heart be *acceptable* in your sight,
O LORD, my rock and my redeemer.
Psalm 19:14

We have already alluded to the right goal of worship, and although a more comprehensive definition of worship would include many more words and correct, biblical concepts, I propose for this study that the ultimate *goal* of our worship is *to please God*. This concept of pleasing God is a single, unifying thread in all of Scripture in regard to worship. Worship that is wrong displeases Him; Worship that is right pleases Him.

Pleasing God in Scripture

I have put together a long list of Scripture passages that show this unifying thread. The complete list is located in the appendix because it is too long to include here. For now we'll just look at a sampling. The point is that pleasing God is not a principle drawn from an isolated verse or two taken out of context. It is a consistent, prevalent theme that runs from the beginning to the end of God's Word. It is repeated over and over and over again. Here are some examples:

> Burn the whole ram on the altar. It is a burnt offering to the LORD. It is a *pleasing aroma*, a food offering to the LORD.
>
> Exodus 29:18

In my English Standard Version Bible, as the Law is laid out in Exodus, Leviticus, and Numbers, the phrase "pleasing aroma" is used thirty-seven times in reference to sacrifices properly offered.

Numerous other passages speak of God's "delight," such as:

> Then will *you delight* in right sacrifices, in burnt offerings and whole burnt offerings; then bulls will be offered on your altar.
>
> Psalm 51:19

Then there are verses that in the ESV translation convey the idea of God's "acceptance." For example:

> And when anyone offers a sacrifice of peace offerings to the LORD to fulfill a vow or as a freewill offering from the herd or from the flock, to be *accepted* it must be perfect; there shall be no blemish in it.
>
> Leviticus 22:21

We can further understand what pleases Him by noting what He "requires" or expects:

> He has told you, O man, what is good; and what does the LORD *require* of you but to do justice, and to love kindness, and to walk humbly with your God?
>
> Micah 6:8

And here is a sampling of verses that refer to "pleasing" God, or that use similar language:

Whatever is needed, . . . let that be given to them . . . [so] that they may offer *pleasing sacrifices* to the God of heaven and pray for the life of the king and his sons.

Ezra 6:9–10

May he remember all your offerings and *regard with favor* your burnt sacrifices!

Psalm 20:3

May my meditation *be pleasing* to him, for I rejoice in the LORD.

Psalm 104:34

Go up to the hills and bring wood and build the house, that I may *take pleasure* in it and that I may be glorified, says the LORD.

Haggai 1:8

Then the offering of Judah and Jerusalem will *be pleasing* to the LORD as in the days of old and as in former years.

Malachi 3:4

For am I now seeking the *approval* of man, or of God?

Galatians 1:10

Try to discern what is *pleasing* to the Lord.

Ephesians 5:10

I have received full payment, and more. I am well supplied, having received from Epaphroditus the gifts you sent, a fragrant offering, a sacrifice *acceptable and pleasing* to God.

Philippians 4:18

This is good, and it is *pleasing* in the sight of God our Savior.

1 Timothy 2:3

> When he said above, "You have *neither
> desired nor taken pleasure* in sacrifices and offerings
> and burnt offerings and sin offerings" (these are
> offered according to the law).
>
> Hebrews 10:8

> Do not neglect to do good and to share what
> you have, for such sacrifices are *pleasing to God.*
>
> Hebrews 13:16

And many more verses like this are listed in the appendix. In contrast, you could do word searches all day long and not find *any* passages mentioning that worship should be *"pleasing to the worshiper"* or be *"acceptable to the worshiper."* Worship is never seen as an encounter in which the feelings or preferences of the worshiper are issues at all.

Can the worshiper ultimately be pleased in worship? Of course. The psalmist said, "I was glad when they said to me, 'Let us go to the house of the LORD'" (Ps. 122:1). But that is a *result*—not a *goal* or an *aim* or a *purpose.* Certainly God can and will bless us as we worship rightly. The Bible often says that we will know joy and gladness as we worship. (Hang with me until our last chapter where we'll discuss that.) But worship can also be tough. If we evaluate worship based on our own fulfillment or if we come seeking our own gratification, we are aiming at pleasing ourselves—the wrong goal. We come to please *Him,* and then we trust Him for the results. The psalmist says, "Delight yourself in the LORD, and he will give you the desires of your heart" (Ps. 37:4). We seek Him first; then after that we receive favor from His hand.

Are you convinced? If so, then the next step is to figure out the *how.* What can we do exactly to please God in our worship? What does that look like? What can I change in order to get past my self-absorption and win the battle against culture and sin and make my goal the sole purpose of pleasing Him? Is it just a matter of singing louder, or what exactly are we talking about?

Pleasing God and Worship Style

There are many clues in the Scripture passages here and in the appendix. We'll look more closely at some of those. But I'll tell you this right now, it isn't the form of worship or the *externals* of worship or a particular style of worship that pleases God. Jesus made it clear in His conversation with the woman at the well that He wasn't much concerned with issues of form:

> The woman said to him, "Sir, I perceive that you are a prophet. Our fathers worshiped on this mountain, but you say that in Jerusalem is the place where people ought to worship." Jesus said to her, "Woman, believe me, the hour is coming when neither on this mountain nor in Jerusalem will you worship the Father. You worship what you do not know; we worship what we know, for salvation is from the Jews. But the hour is coming, and is now here, when the true worshipers will worship the Father in spirit and truth, for the Father is seeking such people to worship him. God is spirit, and those who worship him must worship in spirit and truth."
>
> John 4:19–24

The woman asked about the *where* of worship: Mount Gerizim or Jerusalem? Which is the right place to worship? Jesus went straight to the meaning of true worship, and in so doing communicated that God isn't all that interested in matters of form. God doesn't care about *where* worship happens or in what style or in any other cultural preference. God doesn't care about the externals of worship that were included in the survey in chapter 2. That's not the stuff that pleases or displeases Him. The externals mattered in Leviticus. The Law included precise instructions dealing with how to sacrifice properly, how to handle the ark correctly, and many other issues of form. But Jesus came to fulfill the Law; He became the perfect sacrifice. The point of the form has now been completed in the person of Jesus; the rules have been superseded by a relationship. Even in the Old Testament, in the midst of the rules, God clearly declared that He desires justice, righteous living (Amos 5), purity, goodness (Isaiah 1), love, and an intimate relationship (Hosea 6) more than the sacrifices and trappings of insincere worship. The form just helped them get there.

The Cain and Abel incident points to heart issues rather than form issues. And heart issues in worship became even more important with the coming of Jesus. He became our great High Priest. There is no longer a third-party intermediary. The veil is torn, we have a new intimacy with God, we have the indwelling Spirit, and we can worship "in spirit and truth" (John 4:23–24). What does that mean? In terms of the *truth*, we understand that God's Word is truth and that Jesus Himself is "the way, the truth, and the life" (John 14:6). Worshiping in *spirit* is a little tougher to understand. It refers to the capacity of our human spirit—the part of us that operates in the spiritual realm—to have a personal relationship with God, who is Spirit. Jesus was saying that worship is centered in relationship. The Father is seeking those whose worship is centered around a dynamic, intimate, and life-changing relationship with God through the blood of Jesus and the power of the indwelling Spirit.

The Bible tells us what pleases God in our worship, and it has little to do with *form*. This book isn't about worship style, because that doesn't matter. Sorry. Or maybe that's a relief. We can worship under a tree in Africa with drums and chants. We can worship in a house church in Asia with a guitar. We can worship in a cathedral with pipe organ, stained glass, robes, and Bach. We can worship with praise band, raised hands, dancing, and instruments. Those aren't God's concerns; He doesn't care. God's issues are heart issues and the values we attach to our relationship with Him.

We know this down deep, and here's some proof. If you and I were on a mission trip, we would gladly and enthusiastically enter into a cross-cultural worship experience that might be radically different from what we are accustomed to back home. We would love worshiping with the indigenous people of some remote locale, wouldn't we? We wouldn't care about the language barrier, the native instruments, the chanting style, their dress, the primitive meeting area, or any of that. We would love it. Taken to that extreme, we would be quick to recognize that our worship style differences are cultural and that there is unity with Christians around the world based solely on the blood of Jesus. We would come home talking about the wonderful worship experience we had on a riverbank, in a house church, or outside under a tree with strange music, exotic dress, and expressive dancing. So how important could form be? It's not. Style is an issue here at home only because of our immature self-focus. God has bigger, more important concerns.

Summary

As we think about our narcissistic surroundings and the ways in which we are influenced to seek our own pleasure in worship, the Romans 12 passage quoted earlier takes on new clarity:

> Don't copy the behavior and customs of this world, but let God transform you into a new person by changing the way you think. Then you will learn to know God's will for you, which is good and *pleasing* and perfect.
>
> Romans 12:2, NLT

That's all of it right there in a nutshell. We face tremendous pressure from society to think a certain way—a self-absorbed, self-centered, needy, selfish, and narcissistic way. This is rampantly evident in our corporate worship as we evaluate everything according to our likes and dislikes and

37

whether or not we are pleased. That is worldly. We can't fall for this anymore. We need to let God transform us and change the way we think. We need to shoot for the right goal, give up our worldly infatuation with self, and discover what pleases Him. Over and over in Scripture we see that pleasing God is the standard for worship. That is right worship. That is the real issue. That is our goal.

Questions to Think About

1. Is worship style still a dividing issue at your church? Should it be? How can you help your church get past the conflict?
2. Do you have other critical attitudes about aspects of the worship at your church? Are these attitudes rooted in what you want or in what is pleasing to God?
3. If someone asked you, "How was the worship today?" how would you respond? If someone asked you, "Was God pleased in your worship today?" how would you respond? Which is the better question?

4

Pleasing God by Worshiping Together

For the LORD takes pleasure in his people.
Psalm 149:4

Understanding the *goal* of our worship comes first. Now we need to figure out how to reach that goal. How do we kick the ball the right way? Be warned: aiming at the right goal could lead to a change in the way you approach corporate worship. That has been the case in my own life as I try to live out the very principles that I am writing about.

The following chapters present nine values for corporate worship gleaned from Scripture that will steer us in the right direction. Pursuing these values will help us aim at the right goal in our corporate worship: pleasing God. Why *corporate* worship in particular? That is what the first value is all about—worshiping together.

Meanings of "Worship"

It is helpful to understand that the term "worship" has varied meanings and usages. There are different terms in the Hebrew and Greek that are translated as the English word "worship" in Scripture. John Frame explains that most commonly, the Hebrew term *shachah* and the Greek term *proskuneo* literally mean "bowing" or "bending the knee"—the idea of paying homage or honoring the worth of someone else, which is also the connotation of our English term "worship," which is derived from "worth." A second set of words, primarily the Hebrew *abodah* and the Greek *latreia*, are terms that refer to service or labor, as in the service rendered by Old Testament priests.[5]

In addition, there is a narrow usage of the term "worship" that refers to a specific act—that of paying homage or bowing the knee before someone. For example, the wise men "saw the child with Mary his mother, and they fell down and worshiped him" (Matt. 2:11). This was a single event, a specific act of worship. Then there is a very broad sense in which we use the term "worship." It has become common in recent years to speak of "whole-life worship." That is to say that our entire lives are acts of worship, including all that we do, say, think, and are. Paul says to the Colossians, "And whatever you do, in word or deed, do everything in the name of the Lord Jesus, giving thanks to God the Father through him" (Col. 3:17). All that we do should be for the glory of God. The band Casting Crowns captures this desire in their song "Lifesong" with the words, "May my lifesong sing to You."[6] Harold Best has written a great book about whole-life worship entitled *Unceasing Worship*[7] as has Louie Giglio, writing *The Air I Breathe: Worship as a Way of Life*.[8] These are great books.

But corporate worship is different than both the narrow, specific acts of worship and the broad sense of living lives of worship. It is unique. I ask my class, "If a fellow Christian asked you why he or she needs to come to church to worship, how would you respond?" I typically get good answers about the body of Christ, mutual support, and a discussion of the Hebrews passage, "Let us consider how to stir up one another to love and good works, *not neglecting to meet together*, as is the habit of some, but encouraging one another, and all the more as you see the Day drawing near" (Heb. 10:24–25).

For years that was the passage I would have used to answer that question. But those verses are focused more on encouraging each other than on meeting to worship together— related and relevant, but not compelling. Those verses alone didn't seem to me to be enough to justify our centuries-old traditions of gathering together to worship. Even as a worship pastor, I didn't feel I had a really good answer as to why we should gather to worship. Some Christians, in fact, don't see the need to worship corporately. I know several families who worship on their own and apart from a church family. Others of us gather to worship, but it's not a high value. We miss weeks, we're often late, and we sit way in the back. I think that we innately sense that it's the right thing to do, but the reasons are rarely articulated, so it's a rather hazy feeling.

I want to present a different way of thinking about corporate worship. I believe that our gathering and worshiping as a community of believers is very important to Jesus Christ. The simple act of gathering is the first step toward pleasing Him.

The Church as the Bride of Christ

I read a book way back when I was in college entitled *Destined for the Throne*, by Paul Billheimer. It was an intriguing book, and I've kept this particular paragraph handy over the years:

> The human race was created in the image and likeness of God for one purpose: to provide an eternal companion for the Son. After the fall and promise of redemption through the promised Messiah, Israel was born and nurtured in order to bring in the Messiah. And the Messiah came for one intent and only one: to give birth to His Church, thus to obtain His Bride. The Church, then—the called-out body of redeemed humankind—turns out to be the central object, the

goal, not only of mundane history but of all that God has been doing in all realms, from all eternity.[9]

Billheimer is taking a step back to get a very broad perspective of God's purposes for all of history, and he summarizes it all in three sentences. He says that the crux of all of history and all of creation is this ultimate union of Jesus Christ and the Church. Here is the biblical account of that union:

> Then I heard what seemed to be the voice of a great multitude, like the roar of many waters and like the sound of mighty peals of thunder, crying out, "Hallelujah! For the Lord our God the Almighty reigns. Let us rejoice and exult and give him the glory, for the marriage of the Lamb has come, and his Bride has made herself ready; it was granted her to clothe herself with fine linen, bright and pure"—for the fine linen is the righteous deeds of the saints.
>
> Revelation 19:6–8

Culminating in a great wedding feast, the picture is that of God the Father purposing from time eternal to provide "an eternal companion for the Son," as Billheimer phrases it. That's a little strange for us to think about because it seems to suggest that Christ somehow has a need for companionship. But *need* is not the point. God does not *need* a companion. As Paul explained at the Areopagus, God is absolutely self-sufficient, "for he has no needs" (Acts 17:25, NLT). Nor is He somehow relationally lacking. Jesus's prayer in John 17 shows the fully sufficient love and fellowship that has always existed among the Trinity. Jesus says to the Father, "Bring me into the glory we shared before the world began" (John 17:5, NLT), and later He adds, "You loved me even before the world began!" (John 17:24, NLT). There was and is and always will be perfect love and companionship in the Trinity. God does not *need* additional companionship. But in His sovereignty He has *chosen* to do this. He is sovereign, and He does whatever He wills whether we fully understand it or not. This is the plan He made, and He will carry it out, and in His wisdom He will ultimately bring glory to Himself through the completion of the plan. This is just one of many mysteries about God. Who can know His mind?

The plan has been to provide an eternal companion for Christ, and that companion is the Church. That's the point of creation, redemption, sanctification, and the coming glorification of the Church. It's the point of our existence. We were created so that we could become the Church and enter into an eternal relationship of love with the Lamb of God. It may not be a fair to try to rate the purposes of the local church, but from this perspective, everything we do is done in light of that relationship. We save souls to bring the bride to completion. We teach, grow, and mature to prepare the bride for the wedding day so that we will be pure and spotless. Everything our churches do should be to prepare the Church for the completion of God's plans: the union of the Groom and the bride. And then God will receive glory. That's what Paul is referring to when He talks about explaining God's plan that has been kept secret from the beginning.

> God has now revealed to us his mysterious plan regarding Christ—a plan to fulfill his own good pleasure. And this is the plan: At the right time he will bring everything together under the authority of Christ—everything in heaven and on earth. Furthermore, *because we are united with Christ*, we have received an inheritance from God, for he chose us in advance, and he makes everything work out according to his plan.
>
> Ephesians 1:9–11, NLT

> I was chosen to explain to everyone this mysterious plan that God, the Creator of all things, had kept secret from the beginning. God's purpose in all this was to *use the church* to display his wisdom in its rich variety to all the unseen rulers and authorities in

the heavenly places. This was his eternal plan, which he carried out through Christ Jesus our Lord.

Ephesians 3:9–11, NLT

God, in His wisdom, knew that it would be hard for us to understand this and to grasp the nature of the relationship between Christ and His Church, so He provided a metaphor in His Word to help us. God's Word actually provides many metaphors to help us understand different aspects of the Church. The Church as Christ's body, for example, helps us understand how we fit together and *function* together. But there is a metaphor to help us understand specifically the mystery of the *relationship* between Christ and the Church, and it is the metaphor of marriage. In Paul's letter to the Ephesians he states, "As the Scriptures say, 'A man leaves his father and mother and is joined to his wife, and the two are united into one.' This is a great mystery, but *it is an illustration of the way Christ and the church are one*" (Eph. 5:31–32, NLT).

There are other usages of this illustration in Scripture. As seen already, Revelation 19 describes the union at the wedding feast of the Lamb, and chapters 21–22 continue to expand our understanding of the future role of the Church as Christ's bride. Isaiah alludes to the Messiah as a groom and His people as a bride. In addition, the prophet Hosea was called to wed a prostitute in order to illustrate the relationship between God—the faithful husband—and God's people—the unfaithful wife. Here are some of Hosea's words, using this metaphor to describe Israel's future:

> "When that day comes," says the LORD, "*you will call me 'my husband'* instead of 'my master.' . . . *I will make you my wife forever*, showing you righteousness and justice, unfailing love and compassion. I will be faithful to you and make you mine, and you will finally know me as the LORD."
>
> Hosea 2:16, 19–20, NLT

We can track the metaphor even further in God's Word. I see a list of parallels linking the wedding customs two thousand years ago in Jesus's part of the world with our relationship with Christ *(See Figure 3.1).*

Marriage Customs in Jesus' Time	Our Relationship with Christ
In ancient culture, a couple entered a period of betrothal preceding their marriage. Betrothal was more than a promise of marriage; it was an initiation of marriage.	"I am jealous for you with the jealousy of God himself. *I promised you as a pure bride* to one husband—Christ" (2 Cor. 11:2l, NLT).
The groom paid a price to the father or brother of the bride to purchase his bride.	"The Spirit is God's guarantee that he will give us the inheritance he promised and that *he has purchased us* to be his own people" (Eph. 1:14, NLT).
The groom left his bride to go prepare a home for her.	"I am going to prepare a place for you. ... When everything is ready, I will come and get you, so that you will always be with me where I am" (John 14:2–3, NLT).

Figure 3.1 (a)

45

Marriage Customs in Jesus' Time	Our Relationship with Christ
The groom returned for his bride and together they proceeded to their new home with great celebration.	"For the Lord himself will come down from heaven with a commanding shout, with the voice of the archangel, and with the trumpet call of God. First, the Christians who have died will rise from their graves. Then, together with them, we who are still alive and remain on the earth will be caught up in the clouds to meet the Lord in the air. Then we will be with the Lord forever" (1 Thess. 4:16–17, NLT).
The bride was cleansed and prepared for marriage with a ceremonial bath.	"He [Christ] gave up His life for her [the church] to make her holy and clean, *washed by the cleansing of God's word.* He did this to present her to himself as a glorious church without a spot or wrinkle or any other blemish. Instead, she will be holy and without fault" (Eph. 5:25–27, NLT).

Figure 3.1(b)

Marriage Customs in Jesus' Time	Our Relationship with Christ
The marriage ceremony took place and the bride was presented to the groom. This was followed by the wedding feast and eventually the consummation of the marriage in the bridal chamber.	"'For the time has come for the wedding feast of the Lamb, and his bride has prepared herself. She has been given the finest white linen to wear.' For the fine linen represents the good deeds of God's holy people." (Rev. 19: 7–8, NLT).

Figure 3.1 (c)

I would go so far as to say that God put in place the institution of marriage, the joining of man and wife, for the very purpose of showing us the nature of His relationship with the Church. We are Christ's betrothed. We've been promised. We have a Groom who loves us, has purchased us, is preparing a home for us, and is coming back to get us. This is a powerful biblical picture. So it is that Paul says we should study marriage, this "great mystery" in Paul's words, to better comprehend the relationship between Christ and His Church.

When Becky and I were engaged twenty-four years ago, we spent as much time together as we could. Our relationship was more important than any other earthly thing—it still is. We wanted our relationship to grow and deepen. We still do. We wanted to learn how to express love for each other in rich and meaningful ways. We still do. We wanted to devote the time and effort needed to build our relationship. We still do. We wanted to understand commitment, and "leaving and cleaving," and "becoming one flesh," and communicating well, and loving unconditionally and sacrificially, and everything else that a godly marriage entails. We still do. This is the stuff that constitutes marriage, and Paul says this is the stuff that should help us understand our corporate relationship with Christ. These parallels could supply material for many sermons.

The Bride, the Groom, and Corporate Worship

We are in a *betrothal* period. We are Christ's promised bride, waiting for His physical return and our ultimate marriage with Him that will fulfill God's plan. But we are not fully separated from our Groom, even now we abide in Him (John 15:1–11) and are filled with His indwelling Spirit. We are His temple (another metaphor) in which He dwells. So how do we relate to Him now? How, where, and when is this loving relationship practically played out? The answer is *in corporate worship*. This is exactly what corporate worship is: the interaction between a groom and his bride. This is the time that we gather to function as His bride and focus together on our eternal companion, Jesus Christ. Corporate worship is Christ and His intended coming together in love and intimacy, waiting for the day when the relationship finds completion at the wedding feast. Corporate worship is the dialogue that takes place between two who love each other and take delight in each other's presence.

But here's the kicker: I am not Christ's bride and neither are you. It is all of us *together* who are Christ's bride, all of us who have been redeemed by the blood of Jesus Christ, all of us who have received by faith the gift of eternal life, which is offered freely to all who believe. When Christ relates to His bride in worship, He is relating to *us corporately*. It's a relationship that is hard for us to understand because Americans think more in terms of *I* than *we*, and we're proud of it. We don't think in terms of a corporate identity. That seems like socialism, or the Borg Collective in Star Trek. But Scripture is all about *us*—living together, working together,

48

sharing together, growing together, and worshiping together. Scripture speaks over and over again about unity, love for each other, being *one*, and fitting together as a body. We could fill a couple more pages with these references.

It may seem un-American, but it is scriptural. It may seem devaluing of individuals, but again, that is because of our cultural misconceptions. That is a little sad, and it's a challenge to overcome, but eventually, as we grow in Christ, we will find much more worth as an essential part of Christ's Church (1 Cor. 12:27) than in the pursuit of worth just on our own merits. Of course God wants a relationship with you personally. He loves you. But there is a larger picture in which He loves His bride, and that is us *together*.

The Bride as the Local Church

I can hear some of your objections—right across space and time. You might be protesting that gathering as a local church of 1,000, 300, 75, or even 30 doesn't make us the bride of Christ any more than gathering as our own immediate families. Or you might be thinking about the erratic attendance at church and objecting that there doesn't seem to be a sense in which all of Christ's people ever literally end up in the same place. It's true that logistically the bride of Christ won't fully gather until we reach heaven. It might have been possible for the complete Church to gather together for a week or two after Pentecost, but it is no longer. No stadium is big enough, and we're not all alive at the same time anyway. That was technically true after Pentecost as well. So how does gathering as a tiny fraction of the universal Church make us the bride?

Listen to Paul's perspective. He writes with the assumption that the local church, whatever size or shape, acts and functions *as if* it were the complete Church. Paul tells the local Corinthian church that "all of you together are Christ's body" (1 Cor. 12:27, NLT). As far as functioning as the body of Christ, the Corinthians were complete, lacking in nothing

49

(1 Cor. 1:7). They had all the body parts they needed to minister together and do the work of God. Although there were other local churches in Ephesus and Galatia, the Corinthians *were* the body of Christ. That's how they were to think and function together. This shows that in God's design, the local church acts and functions as the whole Church.

Similarly, Paul says to the Corinthians, "I promised you as a pure bride to one husband—Christ" (2 Cor. 11:2). It's the same idea. He is addressing the Corinthian church as if they are *the* bride of Christ—not just a tiny fraction of the complete bride, but *the* bride. So the issue isn't whether we can assemble *all* of the bride to be the bride. We can't. But we can pursue the *value of gathering* and then function as the bride. And there are many other places where Scripture expresses the value of gathering: the verses in Hebrews cited above, the words of Jesus in Matthew 18:20, "Where two or three are gathered in my name," the model of the church in Acts 2 in which they did everything and shared everything together, and more. The early church clearly gathered. And when we gather, however many worship at our church, we become a corporate participant in God's plan for the ages. We become the bride intended for His Son, Jesus Christ.

Summary

We can't trust our feelings on this one. We may not feel like the bride of Christ, the culmination of God's plan for the ages, when we show up for worship. What happens at your church on an average Sunday morning may seem insignificant and dull rather than like a glorious relationship filled with love and anticipation. You may wonder if it matters if you miss a week and go to the beach, the game, or deer hunting. What's the big deal? You haven't missed much. It may feel that way, but try to look beyond how *you* feel about coming to church and try to understand God's perspective on this. The act of believers gathering to worship is meaningful to Jesus because

50

God's eternal plan is for us to be the companion for Jesus Christ. In anticipation of eternity, as best as we can understand it, Christ is a groom wooing His future bride. He is pouring out His love for her and has given His life for her. Just as I desire to be with Becky, so Christ desires to be with us. Our attitude toward gathering for corporate worship, then, should not be determined by how many warm fuzzies we get when we come but rather by our desire to respond to His love and please Him.

Our first response to His love, before we do anything else in worship, is to show up. If it matters to Him, it should matter to us. We can commit to gathering, to being at church for the interaction between the Groom and His bride even if, at first glance, there are no obvious perks for us. We can respond to the love of Jesus by making corporate worship a priority—one of the highest priorities in our lives. We can choose worship over every other schedule conflict, and we can choose to arrive on time and ready. If He desires to meet us, should we do anything less? The psalmist says, "For the LORD takes pleasure in His people" (Ps. 149:4). He loves us so much that He gave His life for us. May we please Him as we respond and eagerly enter into our corporate interaction with Him.

A Parenthetical Note

Because Jesus desires a relationship with *us*, I am very aware, as a worship leader, of personal pronouns in songs we sing in corporate worship. Steve Green's *Antiphonal Praise*, for example, begins with the line, "We worship You, Almighty God," and then a few moments later continues, "And lift our voice to sing Your praise."[10] I especially like the phrase "lift our voice"—we will talk later about a "corporate voice." But as you well know, many of the songs we sing in corporate worship, in fact most of the songs we sing in corporate worship are from a personal point of view and use the pronoun "I." Laurie Klein's song is an example: "I love You, Lord, and I lift my voice."[11]

I have a list of songs that I reference when I start to plan a worship service—the songs we sing most often at our church. The list changes regularly, but looking at it now, there are ninety-eight songs on the list. Sixteen of the songs have no pronouns but are primarily declarations of truth about God. Thirty-two of the songs are from a corporate point of view, using the pronouns *we* and *our*. The remaining fifty songs use the first person *I* and *my*. Am I arguing that in corporate worship we should lose our individual identities, discard all songs sung from a personal point of view, and only express ourselves as a corporate entity? Is it like the unity candles at a wedding—the ceremony in which the couple lights the unity candle and snuffs out their individual candles? (I would keep those lit!) No, I am not arguing that. In fact, biblical corporate worship is intensely personal. The book of Psalms has historically been used as a hymnbook for corporate worship, and the Psalms are very personal—expressing the whole range of human experience and emotion at a very intimate level.

But here's what happens in corporate worship. You can see it well in Psalm 34.

> *I* will praise the LORD at all times.
> *I* will constantly speak his praises.
> *I* will boast only in the LORD;
> let all who are helpless take heart.
> Come, let *us* tell of the LORD's greatness;
> let *us* exalt his name together.
>
> Psalm 34:1–3, NLT

David begins the first three lines with the personal pronoun. For example, "*I* will praise the Lord at all times." Then he switches to the corporate pronoun: "Come, let *us* tell of the Lord's greatness; let *us* exalt his name together." Our corporate worship flows out of the contributions of every person in the assembly who has been redeemed by the blood of Jesus. It combines the unique offerings of each individual into a concerted expression of love from Christ's beloved bride. What we bring to corporate worship is the expressions of our own hearts, our experiences, our struggles, our joys, and all our thoughts and emotions. Then we take our personal expressions and express them *together*. We speak both as *I* and *we*. We join our individual hearts and *agree* that God is worthy of worship. We become Christ's bride corporately because each of us individually has been redeemed by His blood. Because of His work in each of our separate lives, we can become His united people, joining together with one voice to give praise and glory to God, the Father of our Lord Jesus Christ.

Questions to Think About

1. Do you look at coming to worship at church from your perspective or from God's perspective?
2. Is it a little hard to accept that you are *part* of something bigger—the bride of Christ? Do you feel it devalues your individual worth? Does pride become an issue in this discussion?
3. Are you willing to commit to meeting Christ as His bride—making the effort to arrive at church every week, eager and early and putting corporate worship ahead of anything else you do?

5

Pleasing God
by Worshiping with
Authenticity

Woe to you, scribes and Pharisees, hypocrites!
For you clean the outside of the cup and the plate,
but inside they are full of greed and self-indulgence.
Matthew 23:25

Committing to showing up is a big first step. I believe that
decision alone has great value in God's eyes and is
pleasing to Him because of His desire to relate with His
gathered people. But it is just a first step. What's next as we
desire to please God in our worship? What do we do when we
show up? Well actually, we aren't there yet. There is more to
talk about before we even enter the room. First let's look at a
few verses, and notice the highlighted words:

> But let him who boasts boast in this, that *he
> understands and knows me*, that I am the LORD who
> practices steadfast love, justice, and righteousness
> in the earth. For in these things I delight, declares
> the LORD.
>
> Jeremiah 9:24

"Will the LORD be pleased with thousands of rams, with ten thousands of rivers of oil? Shall I give my firstborn for my transgression, the fruit of my body for the sin of my soul?" He has told you, O man, what is good; and what does the LORD require of you but to do justice, and to love kindness, and *to walk humbly with your God?*

Micah 6:7–8

Walk in a manner worthy of the Lord, fully pleasing to him, bearing fruit in every good work and *increasing in the knowledge of God.*

Colossians 1:10

I want you to show love, not offer sacrifices. *I want you to know me more than I want burnt offerings.*

Hosea 6:6, NLT

Worship that Is a Farce

God's pleasure in our worship is predicated by our knowledge of God and our relationship with Him. In fact, in light of Jesus's condemnation of the Pharisees, I would strengthen that statement and say that our worship doesn't stand a chance of pleasing God if our personal relationship with Christ is estranged or if that relationship is not authentic. Let's look again at Jesus's words to the religious teachers.

The Pharisees and teachers of religious law asked him, "Why don't your disciples follow our age-old tradition? They eat without first performing the hand-washing ceremony." Jesus replied, "You hypocrites! Isaiah was right when he prophesied about you, for he wrote, *'These people honor me with their lips, but their hearts are far from me. Their worship is a farce,* for they teach man-made ideas as commands from God.' For you ignore God's law and substitute your own tradition."

Mark 7:5–8, NLT

On the outside, these guys were active, correct worshipers—devout, religious, saying the right words, and doing the right things. Western culture has few connections to the traditions of ancient Jewish culture, but we do still have our notions of what constitutes acceptable religiosity. Take me, for example. Since I grew up in a churched family, it's been easy to live the church culture. I've been surrounded by good family, good teaching, and good friends. I've always been involved in church activities and service. I've never rebelled. I've done the right things and said the right words. I went to a Christian college and seminary. I've been a pastor for nineteen years. If I avoid scandal and continue doing and saying the right things, most will continue to assume an acceptable level of spirituality in my life.

The truth is, no one really knows what goes on deep in my heart. Now I'm not talking about disbelief or a turning from faith; that would be another kind of deception for someone in my role as a worship pastor. Neither am I talking about unconfessed sin. (We'll tackle that topic in another chapter.) I'm just talking about proximity to God. How close to or how distant from God am I? Am I intimate with Him? Am I absorbing His words and hearing His voice speaking into my life every day? Am I living in the power of His Spirit as I try to be Christ-like in my thoughts, words, and actions? Am I consciously trying to please Him in everything I do? Am I living in obedience, submitting my entire self to Him?

God spoke to Moses "as a man speaks to his friend" (Exod. 33:11); David was a man after God's heart (Acts 13:22); Daniel was "very precious to God" (Dan. 10:11, 19, NLT). Is there a sense at all in which God would consider me a close friend? We know what it takes to be a close friend—time, honesty, love, loyalty, and on and on. Do I bring these things to my relationship with God? No one else really knows my heart in this way. Close friends might know me a little more than most. Becky knows me more than anyone. But if I wanted to, I could fool all of them, at least for a time. I could be quite far from God and maybe get away with it by continuing to function in our church culture—doing and saying all the right things.

It's not that crazy a notion to imagine Pharisees in our churches every Sunday. I often wonder how many churchgoers are fooling other believers each week. They attend church, they sing songs in worship, they might even be involved in ministry, but deep inside there is a great distance between them and God. What about you? The outside looks just fine, but in reality is the inside far from God?

Of course God knows. "For the LORD sees not as man sees: man looks on the outward appearance, but the LORD looks on the heart" (1 Sam. 16:7). "For he knows the secrets of the heart" (Ps. 44:21). It is God "who tests the righteous, who sees the heart and the mind" (Jer. 20:12). It was Jesus who recognized what the Pharisees were like on the inside: "For you are like whitewashed tombs, which outwardly appear beautiful, but within are full of dead people's bones and all uncleanness. So you also outwardly appear righteous to others, but within you are full of hypocrisy and lawlessness" (Matt. 23:27–28). God takes one look at a worshiper walking into church (figuratively speaking) and determines whether the worshiper is a close friend or someone whose heart is far away. If far away, his or her words and actions in worship don't match reality. The worshiper is faking a level of relationship with God that isn't true. He or she is simply mouthing stuff; worship is a farce.

Are any of us walking in perfect intimacy with God all the time? No, of course not. But the point is that we can't ignore God all week then walk into church, give Him some token attention, and expect to please Him. We can't disrespect the relationship for an extended time and then, at our whim, expect it to be suddenly great. We can't tune out His voice all week and then expect to clearly hear Him in worship. We can't close our mind to His thoughts Sunday afternoon through Saturday night and then suddenly understand His Word on

Sunday morning. You can't close your spiritual eyes all week and then honestly sing, "Open the eyes of my heart, Lord, I want to see You," as soon as the music starts at church. Our relationship with God needs to be 24/7, and it simply finds an expanded expression when we gather with others at your worship gathering. If our relationship with God is really 1/1 (just one hour/just one day), there isn't much of a connection. We won't please Him that way; that's not His idea of a meaningful relationship.

Do you do Facebook? I don't, but my wife does. Becky keeps up with current relationships through Facebook, but she has also reconnected with many old friends. She really enjoys it. Maybe you do too. I'm not quite as enthusiastic. Occasionally one of *my* old friends will find me through Becky's account. How does that work? I'll get an email and trade a couple notes with polite chit-chat, but where do you go from there? In some cases, I haven't seen the friend, maybe I haven't even *thought* about the friend, for thirty years. How meaningful can a conversation be? I don't know the person anymore. I suppose that over several emails we could get reconnected and reestablish the friendship, which could be good, but just fishing out there for an old name you recognize seems rather goofy to me. Call me grumpy. One or two emails and we'll talk in another thirty years. See ya!

It's the same thing for inauthentic worshipers. One or two songs, Lord, and see you next week. On Facebook at least we acknowledge the time and distance. In worship, we pretend a closeness that doesn't exist. Quite pointless, and from His perspective, a *farce*.

Pursuing Authenticity

The remedy is not rocket science; you know this well. Pleasing God in our worship entails cultivating hearts that are close to Him. If we draw near to God, "He will draw near to you" (James 4:8). God says through the prophet Jeremiah that "you will seek me and find me, when you seek me with all your heart" (Jer. 29:13). These verses suggest to me that as far as intimacy with God in the Christian life is concerned, the initiative is largely up to me. Certainly there are times when God takes the initiative and reaches into my heart to shake me up, and this can happen in worship. But even after these reminders, I will choose how close I am consistently living to God. If I pursue God, in His mercy He will respond and draw near to me. If I turn elsewhere to pursue the things of this world, God will not just tag along behind keeping up with me. That's not the way it works with the almighty, omnipotent, King of the universe.

We draw near to God by, first of all, reading His Word. This is how we know God because the Bible contains His very words. We hear God and our hearts draw close to Him as we read, study, and meditate on His Word. This has to happen in the life of a Christian who desires to please Him in worship. Perhaps you have never developed this habit. Like any other discipline, it can be rough going for a while. Many of us start Scripture reading plans—maybe as a New Year's resolution— and then fizzle out in Leviticus somewhere. I recommend figuring out a plan in which you read a little from different parts of the Bible each day rather than starting in Genesis and plowing straight ahead. But I discovered long ago that you can get through the initial, hard period and find that you have indeed formed a habit—that daily Scripture reading has become a necessary part of your day that you never want to miss. And once you are in the habit, your life changes. It's inevitable. If you are opening your eyes, your mind, and your heart to God's Word every single day, it will make you a new person. You'll be "transformed by the renewal of your mind" (Rom. 12:2) and know the Spirit's work in your life in ever-increasing ways. "So shall my word be that goes out from my mouth; it shall not return to me empty, but it shall accomplish that which I purpose, and shall succeed in the thing for which I sent it" (Isa. 55:11).

In addition, of course, is the discipline of prayer. Having a great prayer life has been a life-long challenge for me—and it still is. My mind wanders big-time. But I am committed to devoting time to pray every day. How else can I be a friend of God and know His heart? If you struggle like me, experiment with some structured prayers that can guide you and keep your mind in the game. Many resources are available. I personally use the Lord's Prayer as a guide or template. The disciples asked Jesus how to pray, and He gave them the Lord's Prayer. I figure that if it was good enough for Peter, James, and John, it's good enough for me. Then there are a variety of additional disciplines that can help you find and maintain a dynamic closeness with God, such as Scripture memorization, journaling, fasting, and meditating.

But a life lived close to God doesn't just happen. Close friendships don't just happen. Great marriages don't just happen. We have to want it, and we have to go for it. Without authenticity in our relationship with God, our worship has questionable value. We are listening to words that we have already decided to ignore. We are mouthing truths that are not realities in our life. We are ostensibly participating in an intimate conversation with someone with whom we are not intimate. Jesus said this kind of worship is a farce.

Summary

God told Isaiah to confront His people about their inauthentic worship. He wanted to get their attention with "the voice of a trumpet blast" (Isa. 58:1, NLT). He wanted His people to clearly understanding why He was not pleased with their behavior and their words. Isaiah 58 is a powerful chapter about worshiping God rightly:

> Shout with the voice of a trumpet blast.
> Shout aloud! Don't be timid.

> Tell my people Israel of their sins!
> > Yet they act so pious!
> They come to the Temple every day
> > and seem delighted to learn all about me.
> They act like a righteous nation
> > that would never abandon the laws of its God.
> They ask me to take action on their behalf,
> > pretending they want to be near me.
> "We have fasted before you!" they say.
> > "Why aren't you impressed?
> We have been very hard on ourselves,
> > and you don't even notice it!"
>
> "I will tell you why!" I respond.
> > "It's because you are fasting to please yourselves.
> Even while you fast,
> > you keep oppressing your workers.
> What good is fasting
> > when you keep on fighting and quarreling?
> This kind of fasting
> > will never get you anywhere with me.
> You humble yourselves
> > by going through the motions of penance,
> > bowing your heads
> > like reeds bending in the wind.
> You dress in burlap
> > and cover yourselves with ashes.
> Is this what you call fasting?
> > Do you really think this will please the LORD?"
>
> Isaiah 58:1–5, NLT

Coming to church can please God, but not if we're hypocrites. Not if we're just acting a part in order to scratch some of our own itches or to look good. Our relationship with God must be real before we enter the room. Only then will we be able to please God in worship.

Questions to Think About

1. Have you read God's Word and spent time in prayer today? Yesterday? The day before?
2. Are the things you hear from God on Sunday morning reinforcing the things you have been hearing from God all week? Are the things you say to God on Sunday morning reinforcing the things you have been saying to Him all week?
3. If you heard God greet you when you walked into corporate worship, would He say, "Welcome, friend," or would He say, "Where have you been?" Or even worse, would He say, "Who are you?"

6

Pleasing God by Engaging in Worship

What then, brothers? When you come together,
each one has a hymn, a lesson, a revelation, a
tongue, or an interpretation.
1 Corinthians 14:26

There are several God encounters in Scripture that give us insight into the interaction we should expect as we gather to meet God. John tells of his encounter with Christ in Revelation 1. Moses encountered God in the burning bush in Exodus 3. Isaiah's vision described in the sixth chapter of his book is especially helpful in giving us a model for worship:

> In the year that King Uzziah died I saw the Lord sitting upon a throne, high and lifted up; and the train of his robe filled the temple. Above him stood the seraphim. Each had six wings: with two he covered his face, and with two he covered his feet, and with two he flew. And one called to another and said:
>
> "Holy, holy, holy is the LORD of hosts; the whole earth is full of his glory!"
>
> And the foundations of the thresholds shook at the voice of him who called, and the house was filled

with smoke. And I said: "Woe is me! For I am lost; for I am a man of unclean lips, and I dwell in the midst of a people of unclean lips; for my eyes have seen the King, the LORD of hosts!"

Then one of the seraphim flew to me, having in his hand a burning coal that he had taken with tongs from the altar. And he touched my mouth and said: "Behold, this has touched your lips; your guilt is taken away, and your sin atoned for."

And I heard the voice of the Lord saying, "Whom shall I send, and who will go for us?" Then I said, "Here am I! Send me." And he said, "Go, and say to this people:

"'Keep on hearing, but do not understand; keep on seeing, but do not perceive.' Make the heart of this people dull,
> and their ears heavy,
> and blind their eyes;
> lest they see with their eyes,
> and hear with their ears,
> and understand with their hearts,
> and turn and be healed."

Isaiah 6:1–10

Isaiah's worship encounter with God shows a pattern that can be emulated. It is a dialogue: God spoke, or was revealed, and Isaiah responded. He saw God's holiness and glory, and he responded by recognizing that he was unclean. He confessed his sin, and he received cleansing. He heard God's call to service, and he responded in obedience. Many worship services purposefully emulate this kind of worship conversation. There is interaction; it is a two-way conversation, not a one-sided monologue. Paul offers this prayer for the Romans: "May the God of endurance and encouragement grant you to live in such harmony with one another, in accord with Christ Jesus, that *together you may with one voice* glorify the

God and Father of our Lord Jesus Christ" Romans 15:5–6.✓ "Together with one voice" shows that everyone gathered is participating in the conversation; everyone is involved. And he says to the Corinthians, "When you come together, each one has a hymn, a lesson, a revelation, a tongue, or an interpretation. Let all things be done for building up" (1 Cor. 14:26). Everyone brings something to worship and everyone participates.

Two Corporate Worship Analogies

Søren Kierkegaard observed that corporate worship is treated as if those on the platform are performers and those in the pews are an audience.[12] We've alluded to the fact that we've grown accustomed to the culture of concerts, theater, movies, sporting events, and the like and have come to worship with a similar posture—that of a spectator. Churches even encourage the performer/spectator dynamic by structuring the service like a concert and designing the room like a theater. Some churches have tried to intentionally redress this by designing their worship space differently. I have seen circular arrangements and other worship gatherings in which the worship leaders are placed to the side or even behind the worshipers. These kinds of arrangements can present challenges for technical and production teams, but I think they are well worth considering.

Kierkegaard states, though, that the performer/spectator mindset reveals a misunderstanding of worship. His well-known observation is that *God* is the audience, those of us in the pews are all performers, and the leaders on the platform provide cues for the performance. This is a good analogy, but not perfect. It's better not to think of worship in the context of a *performance* at all. Worship is about relationship and interaction, not performance. But Kierkegaard's point is that the real *action* in worship is on the floor, not the platform.

I prefer a different analogy that makes the same point: I went to Garfield Elementary School in Maywood, Illinois, and Glenn Rivers was in my class. Glenn was a great basketball player even in grade school, and he became an instant star at Proviso East High School. He went on to Marquette University, where he picked up the nickname "Doc," and then he had a successful career in the NBA playing mostly for the Atlanta Hawks. Following his playing days, he coached the Orlando Magic and most recently coaches the Boston Celtics. In 2008 he coached them to the NBA championship, and they came within a game of winning the championship in the 2010 finals. So every time Doc Rivers is on TV, I remind my kids that I knew him in grade school.

The game of basketball, though, is played on the basketball floor. No matter how good a coach Doc is, the results of the game are determined by what happens on the hardwood, not the bench. Doc and his staff provide direction, motivation, and guidance, but he can't score points from the bench. It is the players on the floor who determine the results of the game. It is Kevin Garnett, Paul Pierce, Ray Allen, and Rajon Rondo who have to convert on offense and play defense. The coaches are certainly a factor—they influence the game for better or worse—but the outcome of the game is determined by how well the team plays basketball.

Corporate worship can be compared to a basketball game. Those of us in the pew are the ball players, and the worship leaders are the coach and coaching staff. Can you imagine a basketball team sitting down on the floor to watch the coaches coach? Of course not. But that's exactly what happens in church. Some people come to worship but are virtually inactive while sitting in the pew and watching the coaches. Have we been duped? Have we accepted the notion that what occurs on the platform during our worship is the main thing? Unfortunately, many people believe the platform activity is what defines worship.

Of course basketball is not a perfect analogy either. In corporate worship the leadership is really more like the old-style player/coach playing and coaching at the same time. I think Pete Rose did that. Now don't get me wrong; coaching is important. It was God's idea to designate skilled leaders to facilitate the corporate worship of His people. It was God who included instructions for worship leadership when He gave David the plans for the temple (see 2 Chronicles). Worship leaders perform an important role, and they need to effectively lead—an entire book could be written on that topic. But the real issue for us now is whether worshipers can offer right worship regardless of the quality of the coaching. They are on the floor; they are the action.

The Action in Our Worship

What does that mean? How are we the "action" as we worship—especially when worshipers are often treated as spectators in many of our worship environments? Our personal traditions color how we think about this question. Some of us are very familiar with liturgical worship, which often requires a great deal of involvement from the worshipers: responding, praying, reciting, singing, kneeling, coming forward to receive the Eucharist, giving, standing up, sitting down, etc. There is often criticism that this kind of formal worship is engaging only at a behavioral level and can be rote and mindless. Sure; that can be true in liturgical worship as well as in any kind of worship style. Other charismatic styles of worship typically include a very high level of another kind of engagement: clapping, raising hands, dancing, shouting, speaking in tongues, etc. I hear criticism that this kind of worship is engaging only at the physical and emotional levels. Sure; that is a possibility as well. Both of these forms, though, are commendable in that they at least provide a starting point for the worshiper to engage. On the other hand, it's harder to understand the value of participation in the traditions of many other evangelical churches. I grew up just sitting in the pew, basically listening, standing to sing a few songs, maybe putting money in the offering plate, and taking communion once a month. The options for being part of the action seemed rather limited—sing better or louder, I guess.

So what should engagement ideally look like? How should the action happen in the pew? There is no one-size-fits-all answer. God made each of us and each of our worshiping families unique. But consider how a conversation works: First of all, God speaks, and a participating worshiper should be listening for God's voice. God speaks in a zillion different ways in a worship service. He thunders and He speaks in a still, small voice as He did with Elijah. He speaks through an instrumental piece preceding the service. He speaks through the interaction between fellow worshipers as they have an opportunity to share for a few moments. He speaks through the words of songs, directly through the reading of Scripture, or as worshipers are led in corporate prayer. He speaks through a stained glass window or a video clip, an oil painting or a MediaShout presentation. He speaks in moments of quiet reflection. He speaks through drama or dance or a poem. He speaks through an electric guitar solo. He most certainly speaks through the exposition of His Word. He speaks through the elements of His Table and through the participation of the bread and the cup. He speaks through testimonies. He speaks through the confession of belief in baptisms. He speaks through the church-family interactions as children are dedicated, missionaries are sent out, and leaders are affirmed. And like it or not, He also speaks through church discipline.

But unfortunately, God's voice in all of these elements of a worship service can go unheard. The truth can go sailing right over our heads. We grow accustomed to our particular worship format; it becomes routine and our minds disengage. It's possible to sing songs and say words and listen to sermons without engaging. The engaged worshiper, on the other hand, will be looking and listening for God's words in all of the elements listed above, and more. And God doesn't need a great preacher or great worship leadership to speak to us. He really doesn't. He's bigger than that. It's not an issue of how good our church is. He speaks, and if we listen, we will hear Him. The engaged worshiper will be attuned to every word and every whisper—focused, eager, and even taking notes. The engaged worshiper will not want to miss *anything* that God might reveal of Himself. Whether shouted or whispered, it's God talking. If we want to be this kind of engaged worshiper, the first step is to discipline our eyes, ears, and mind to look and listen for God everywhere.

The model in Isaiah shows us that after God speaks, we are to respond. If we are engaged in worship, we respond by confessing sin as we are confronted with His holiness and glory. We respond by giving praise when we see His greatness. We respond with our joy when we experience His goodness and mercies that are new every morning. We respond with our thanks and gratitude as we remember His works and share at His Table. We respond by giving Him our cares and our honest struggles as we remember His loving kindness and are reminded that His yoke is easy. We respond by giving our gifts as we trust His care and live lives of gratitude. We respond by making decisions to obey and follow as we are challenged by His instructions. We respond by offering our service as we hear His call. We respond by reaching out to touch the lives of our fellow worshipers as we understand His love and His desire for our unity. We respond by interceding for others as we see His power to save and heal. And that's just a start.

If we are engaged in worship, we respond internally with our thoughts and our will focused and attuned. And we respond externally. If clapping and the raising of hands is a scriptural expression of worship, why do we not clap and raise our hands? If Scripture calls us to kneel, and we even sing songs about bowing, why do we not bow?[13] We might say that

Clapping + engaging / raising a hand - things a prayer prompted

we are bowing "in my heart." That's well and good. Certainly we can have an attitude of reverence when we sing of bowing. But I know for sure that the physical act of bowing before God expresses my submission and His reign in my life more than just an internal attitude. Mark 12:30 says to "love the Lord your God with all your heart and with all your soul and with all your mind and with all your strength." The psalmist says, "With my whole being, *body and soul*, I will shout joyfully to the living God" (Ps. 84:2, NLT). This means all of me—every part. It's all connected, and all of the parts reinforce each other, so why would we separate our minds from our bodies or our emotions from our wills?

Our brains have two sides, and rumor has it that some of us favor the side that deals with emotions while others of us favor the side that processes information. Which do you favor? Some of us are more naturally *thinkers*, and some of us are more naturally *feelers*, and that's just the beginning of our personality differences. Different personalities will engage in different ways, but we will also have different challenges as we think about being engaged worshipers.

I am more of a thinker. In addition, I grew up in a rather straitlaced worship environment. There wasn't much emotion expressed, which suited me fine. I have learned, though, that responding to God's grace and love in worship calls for an expression from *all of me*. So, for example, I have learned to raise my hands. It didn't come naturally; I practiced. I learned to clap. I didn't much care for that at first either. At times in our corporate worship I have helped lead our congregation in bowing low to the ground at the feet of Jesus. That was way out my comfort zone. These physical expressions of submission, joy, and supplication have both reinforced what I am *thinking* and have helped me tap into how I am *feeling*. It's all connected. Whatever your natural disposition, you may have to work at getting all cylinders firing. Thinkers need to work on feeling and expressing. Feelers need to work on understanding and processing truth. We should respond with the whole package: our hearts, our souls, our minds, and our strength. "I will sing in the spirit, and I will also sing in words I understand" (1 Cor. 14:15, NLT). If we believe the Isaiah model, each revelation of God will result in some kind of response on our part, and the engaged worshiper will hear God's voice and participate fully in the answer.

Summary

I don't know what this exactly means for you at your church. We face so many cultural pressures in our worship that it is very difficult to figure out how to behave. We have our traditions that dictate what is acceptable and what is not. We want to be guided by God's Word, not by culture, but that doesn't make it easy to change the way we behave in worship. We are quick to be offended, so we worry about offending others. We are quick to be distracted, so we worry about distracting others. It's a shame. But at the core, if we are engaged worshipers, we will purposefully join with those around us in entering into a dialogue with God. As best we can, we will set aside our criticisms, our inhibitions, and all other stuff that hinders us and give ourselves fully to claim a part in whatever thoughts and expressions are corporately being offered as worship. Style doesn't matter. Our preferences are not the issue. Good worship leadership can certainly help, but our participation doesn't depend on that. Engagement is a *choice*, and we can choose to engage in any context that in rooted in truth.

Here's one more observation that may say a lot about your personal willingness to engage in corporate worship. At your church, do the seats in back fill up first? Is there usually room at the front? Does that say anything? Probably.

As a student, Becky was motivated and fully engaged. She wanted to learn, so she took notes, made eye contact with the lecturer, and responded with good facial feedback and body language. And she sat very close to the front. It was part of her desire to engage. When she comes to worship, she brings the same attitude. She heads down to the front to be part of the action. On the other hand, when I was a student I had *no* desire to engage. I covertly did crossword puzzles during lectures. When I showed up for class, I sat far in the back where I folded my arms, slouched in my seat, and barely watched the action with little, if any, personal involvement. So on those rare occasions when I am not leading worship and I come to worship with Becky, my tendency is to want to sit farther back. Old habits. For me it's a little battle, and I have to *decide* to be an engaged participant in worship, and that starts by walking with Becky to the front. That decision in itself establishes an attitude of wanting to hear God and to fully respond to Him.

Do you sit in back? I am not in a position to judge whether you are a spectator or an engaged worshiper, but I did say I was going to get in your face a little bit. Maybe you are doing an Ebert and Roper routine back there. Maybe you are just a critic, with thumbs up or thumbs down as you watch the worship unfold. Or maybe you are fully engaged. It's harder to be fully engaged in the back, but maybe you are pulling it off. Only God knows. But think about it. This could be a very simple, but accurate test of your participation in worship.

This is the value of engagement. If we return to the picture of Christ and His bride, we can see the absurdity of an interaction without two-way communication. Would Christ be pleased if He poured out His love only to be met with stony faces, hard hearts, distracted minds, crossed arms, and silent lips? All loving relationships are predicated on great communication. Worship that pleases God is worship in which each and every worshiper is making every effort to be integrally involved in the dialogue.

The Unbeliever in Worship

On a side note, the unbeliever is the exception. The unbeliever is not redeemed by the blood of Jesus and is not part of His Church, and as such, cannot be part of the interaction between Christ and His bride. Worshipers are to worship "in spirit and in truth." Those who have not yet trusted in Christ do not have the indwelling Spirit and are still in the process of being drawn *to* the Truth. Does this mean that unbelievers are not welcome in the room in which corporate worship is taking place? On the contrary; it can be an incredible opportunity for someone outside the family of God to observe and experience the incredible dynamic of corporate worship. Observing the soul-satisfying interaction between Christ and His bride can create a yearning inside the unbeliever to be included in the relationship. Sally Morgenthaler explored this whole issue some years ago in her book *Worship Evangelism: Inviting Unbelievers into the Presence of God*,[14] but suffice to say that we should *welcome* unbelievers into God's presence. May they glimpse Him and desire to know Him. I have invited non-Christians to play with our worship band or orchestra. If it is a positive experience for them, they will come back, and the greater the chance will be that they will meet Jesus (That's not really theologically sound, but you know what I mean). Paul indicates that an unbeliever should encounter God when entering our places of worship. "But if all prophesy, and an unbeliever or outsider enters, he is convicted by all, he is called to account by all, the secrets of his heart are disclosed, and so, falling on his face, *he will worship God and declare that God is really among you*"(1 Cor. 14:24–25).

May we as believers experience dynamic, life-changing, soul-satisfying worship as we meet and converse with our Groom, and may others observe and desire to be part of Christ's incredibly privileged bride and to be participants in the relationship.

Questions to Think About

1. Were you looking and listening for God the last time you were in corporate worship? What did He say? If He had whispered, would you have heard Him?
2. Did you participate in responding to Him? What did you say? Was it internal? Was it external? How?
3. Are you a spectator at worship gatherings or are you an active, engaged player?

7

Pleasing God by Worshiping in Unity

Only let your manner of life be worthy of the gospel of Christ,
so that whether I come and see you or am absent,
I may hear of you that you are standing firm in one spirit,
with one mind striving side by side for the faith of the gospel.
Philippians 1:27

We are divided in our worship. We are divided by denominations, color, socio-economic status, worship style, age, mind-set, preferences, and anything else that causes me to disagree with you. This must grieve God deeply. It certainly is not His intent for our worship.

Unified Worship in Scripture

Jesus's prayer for believers is that "they will be one, just as you and I are one—Father" (John 17:21). Paul pleads with the Corinthians to "be of one mind, united in thought and purpose" (1 Cor. 1:10, NLT). Here are these verses again as Paul writes to the Romans:

May God, who gives this patience and encouragement, help you live *in complete harmony*

He does NOT TALK of MULTIPLE BRIDES
" TALKS of ONE BRIDE

with each other, as is fitting for followers of Christ Jesus. Then all of you *can join together with one voice,* giving praise and glory to God, the Father of our Lord Jesus Christ.

Romans 15:5–6, NLT

Paul's model for worship mirrors John's vision in Revelation in which all of Christ's bride joins together—every nation, every tongue, grandparents and grandchildren, rich and poor, black and white and every other color or ethnicity. Revelation 4 describes the throne in heaven and the worship surrounding the throne. Verse 4 talks about twenty-four thrones around God's throne and the twenty-four elders seated on these thrones. I have heard it suggested that these twenty-four elders represent the unity of all of God's people—perhaps encompassing Old Testament Israel (the twelve tribes) and the New Testament church (the twelve apostles). The twenty-four elders are joined by the four living creatures.

> [There are] four living creatures, full of eyes in front and behind: the first living creature like a lion, the second living creature like an ox, the third living creature with the face of a man, and the fourth living creature like an eagle in flight. And the four living creatures, each of them with six wings, are full of eyes all around and within, and day and night they never cease to say,
>
> "Holy, holy, holy, is the Lord God Almighty, who was and is and is to come!"
>
> Revelation 4:6–8

In chapter 5, the elders and the four living creatures are joined by angels "numbering myriads of myriads and thousands of thousands, saying with a loud voice, 'Worthy is the Lamb who was slain, to receive power and wealth and wisdom and might and honor and glory and blessing'" (Rev. 5:11–12). And then the elders, the four living creatures and the angels are joined by every other living creature.

> And I heard *every creature in heaven and on
> earth and under the earth and in the sea, and all that
> is in them*, saying, "To him who sits on the throne and
> to the Lamb be blessing and honor and glory and
> might forever and ever!" And the four living creatures
> said, "Amen!" and the elders fell down and worshiped.
> Revelation 5:13–14

Every living creature will join together to worship the Lamb. This is God's intent for worship and a picture of the unity that glorifies and pleases Him. Biblical corporate worship never divides people. Instead, the examples of corporate worship in the Bible show believers drawn together. In addition to this vision in Revelation, there is the worship at the dedication of the temple in 2 Chronicles 5–7 and the worship of the first church in Acts 2. Each instance displays God's people gathering and joining together to meet Him.

Worshiping in Unity Today

Given our divisions in today's worship, is this kind of unity realistic? Will this kind of unity only be realized in the throne room of heaven? Well, things will certainly be different when we arrive at that scene. We will be like Christ (1 John 3:2), and our bodies will be transformed into a glorified state (1 Cor. 15:43). Our natural bodies are now subject to being governed by our selfish wills, whereas our glorified bodies will be fully responsive to the Holy Spirit's guidance. John's account provides evidence that in our "spiritual bodies" (1 Cor. 15:44) we will not encounter the barriers of logistics or language, but even more to the point, we will not encounter the barriers of cultural, racial, generational, or personal preferences. There will be an absence of evil. All of our barriers will fade away as we bow together in the radiance of His glory. There will no longer be any issue of what we prefer or expect. Finding unity in worship is not about the music style, but rather it's about *us*. When *we* are changed, then we will indeed worship together.

But for now, achieving unity in worship sure seems like an uphill battle from where I am sitting. But look again at Paul's prayer:

> May God, who gives this patience and encouragement, help you live in complete harmony with each other—*each with the attitude of Christ Jesus toward the other*. Then all of you can join together with one voice, giving praise and glory to God, the Father of our Lord Jesus Christ.
>
> Romans 15:5–6, NLT, 1st edition

We can experience harmony with each other and join together with one voice, but it is only possible when we have "the attitude of Christ Jesus toward the other." What is this attitude? Philippians 2 describes it vividly:

> Have this mind among yourselves, which is yours in Christ Jesus, who, though he was in the form of God, did not count equality with God a thing to be grasped, but made himself nothing, taking the form of a servant, being born in the likeness of men. And being found in human form, he humbled himself by becoming obedient to the point of death, even death on a cross.
>
> Philippians 2:5–8

Christ's attitude was one of humble, selfless obedience, and that is what is needed for us to worship together in unity. If we come to worship with Christ-like humility and Christ-like selflessness, all our divisions and barriers will melt away. We won't be able to fully achieve this on this earth, but we will when we reach glory. For now it is a process. Paul says that all of us have had that veil removed (a veil that covered our minds regarding truth) so that we can be mirrors that brightly reflect the glory of the Lord. And as the Spirit of the Lord works within us, *we become more and more like him* and reflect his glory even more (2 Cor. 3:18).

We are being sanctified, constantly renewed (Col. 3:10), and drawn nearer to Christ-likeness. As we mature in Christ we are less governed by our selfish wills and are more responsive to the Holy Spirit's guidance. As this happens, we can increasingly find unity in worship. We can let go of biases and expectations and fix our united hearts solely on Christ. There will be fewer and fewer reasons to divide as we realize it's not about the external stuff but instead is about our willingness to selflessly yield our preferences. We can find unity in worship when we let go of the things that aren't crucial and embrace those things that are—the blood of Jesus, the truth of the Word of God, and the power of the risen Christ. We can find unity in worship when we humble ourselves and don't insist on our way, our methods, our style, our procedures, our comfort, our pleasure, and our satisfaction. Unity in worship can come when we act like Jesus Christ and embrace our brothers and sisters in Christ with acceptance and love, no matter how different we are.

Applications for Unity in Worship

I've got an idea for my next book. It's called *Walk to Church*. In that book I will argue that New Testament Christians all had to walk to church (or ride a donkey?), and so should we. We should form churches with other believers who are within walking distance. I will argue that cars are bad when it comes to church membership. Cars allow us to *choose* a church. Who ever said we should be able to choose a church? Where did that idea come from? Who said that church should be a place that agrees with us or gives us what we want, what we "need," or what we prefer? Having choices only enables us to succumb to the values of our world, cater to ourselves, and help ourselves from the church buffet—the giant, customizable religious emporium that we talked about in chapter two. The Galatians, Ephesians, and Colossians had zero options. They gathered with those within walking distance, and then they had

81

to work stuff out and figure out how to live in unity. And shame on them if they couldn't! We often think about this next passage just in terms of "legal disputes," but listen to Paul's strong words in light of any of our church disagreements:

> When one of you has a dispute with another believer, how dare you file a lawsuit and ask a secular court to decide the matter instead of taking it to other believers! Don't you realize that someday we believers will judge the world? *And since you are going to judge the world, can't you decide even these little things among yourselves? Don't you realize that we will judge angels? So you should surely be able to resolve ordinary disputes in this life.* If you have legal disputes about such matters, why go to outside judges who are not respected by the church? I am saying this to shame you. *Isn't there anyone in all the church who is wise enough to decide these issues?* But instead, one believer sues another—right in front of unbelievers!
>
> 1 Corinthians 6:1–6, NLT

Paul says we are going to judge the world, and we are going to judge angels! Can't we resolve our "little things"? Paul wrote to shame the Corinthians. We should be embarrassed, too, when we squabble and divide over small stuff.

It would be much closer to the New Testament model if we walked to church and found unity with neighboring believers based solely on the saving blood of Jesus Christ. There would be many positives: (1) Our church could be a much tighter community. We could actually live with each other in a way that is closer to the Acts 2 model. (2) Our church would probably rely on us more. We would need to identify and use our gifts rather than coming to be pampered at big church as some do. (3) Imagine how much more connected our churches could be to the people and the needs in our neighborhoods. It could be very cool. But we would also be forced to live in unity. Zero options; no church-hopping. What do you think?

It ain't gonna happen. There are indeed valid reasons why Catholics and Baptists don't worship together, so right away there would be a church split, and the process of dividing would just start all over again.

That was my entire book, by the way, so that book ain't gonna happen either. But do you see my point? Unity is not the product of finding the perfect church that is the perfect fit to meet all of our self-perceived needs and criteria. Unity is the result of *each of us* as individuals having the selfless attitude of Christ wherever we find ourselves.

Walking to church may not be the answer, but there are more realistic applications as we face divisions in our worship. First of all, even if you are able to drive a car and choose from twenty different churches, you have to stop church-hopping. In fact, stop at the church you are at right now and commit to never leave. Do you think the church is lacking something—dynamic preaching, exciting youth ministry, moving worship? Paul says to the Corinthians that they "have every spiritual gift you need as you eagerly wait for the return of our Lord Jesus Christ" (1 Cor. 1:7, NLT). Your church is complete. It isn't lacking anything. It just needs *your* commitment, *your* spiritual gifts, *your* financial gifts, *your* prayer and *your* selfless Christ-like attitude. We won't worship in unity by finding a better church. But we will make progress toward worshiping in unity by living, loving, serving and worshiping with those in our church right now. Having said that, there are, sadly, churches that implode (or explode) because of sin. If that is your church, try to be an agent of love, forgiveness, repentance and change. But there times when leaving is necessary, and you do need to worship in a church that fully holds to the truth of God's Word. (We will discuss that more fully in the next chapter.) Far too often, though, we change churches because of our own "needs" and we just want an upgrade.

Second, we should give more thought to divisions of color, denomination, and social class. These are firmly entrenched divisions, but I encourage you to think beyond your comfort zone and look for ways to worship with those unlike you. We could brainstorm for a long time about how to do this. Are there opportunities to partner with another church unlike ours and share worship together? Are there opportunities for us to participate in cross-cultural worship? Are there community efforts that could bring together different worshiping cultures? Are there things our church could do to lessen the barriers for those whose traditions are different? These are all worth pursuing as we desire to please God in our unity.

Third, we can make some better choices in our thinking about worship style. For many of us, the rubber really meets the road when we talk about worship style. Now there are issues of doctrine that explain other divisions in the Church Universal, and we can work to break those down and worship together. But underlying theological differences usually are deeply rooted and not open to compromise. But our divisions over worship *style* are different. They are rooted in self-centeredness, and we haven't always handled the strife in a God-pleasing way.

One of the requirements for students in my class is to interview a worship leader in a church that offers multiple styles of worship. These churches are not hard to find. Over the past decades many churches have responded to the worship conflicts by continuing to offer some sort of *traditional* service and then adding a *contemporary* service, trying to accommodate congregants on both sides of the dispute. This became a very common model. Then, as I've mentioned, ten or fifteen years ago some larger video-venue-based churches expanded this model to offer an even greater variety of worship styles all on the same campus—heavy metal, pop, bluegrass, traditional, whatever. I don't hear about this as much now. Current growth efforts seem to be toward a *multi-site* model, and there seems to be more uniformity in worship style involved in multi-sites, but there are still many churches offering two or more different styles of worship. My students report many interesting comments from worship leaders in these situations. There are some who report satisfaction with the multi-style formula. It "gives people what they want," which leads to church growth and satisfied worshipers. I take exception to that satisfaction, because that doesn't necessarily mean that God is satisfied, which is really the issue. And that's what this book is about. But I am finding that a greater number of worship leaders are expressing dissatisfaction with the multi-style model. I personally think the pendulum is swinging on this. More and more worship leaders talk about the sense that their church is divided and that there is a lack of unity stemming from multiple worship style offerings. Having tried multiple styles for a while, the realization is growing that it comes at the expense of unity.

The issue is a little complicated. Here are a couple points to muddy the waters: (1) Churches often need to add services to accommodate growth. Hallelujah! Adding a service in this situation has nothing to do with style and everything to do with finding available seats. (2) We aren't talking much here about worship leadership, but I believe that worship leaders have a role in finding what I call the "corporate voice." This is the unique expression of a local church that best enables them to communicate with God—to understand His voice and to express themselves in return. John Frame, in his excellent book *Worship in Spirit and Truth: A Refreshing Study of the Principles and Practice of Biblical Worship*, argues, based mostly on 1 Corinthians 14, that worship should be "intelligible." That is to say that style will, and should, change over time so that the language of worship allows worshipers to understand, speak, and engage. Frame says that "if the church takes this principle seriously, it will necessarily encourage changes in musical styles and language in order to communicate with new generations."[15] Of course. I couldn't agree more. We don't worship in Latin anymore because nobody speaks Latin. We don't worship in Swahili when we only speak English. Paul said, "I will pray in the spirit, and I will also pray *in words I understand. I will sing in the spirit, and I will also sing *in words I understand*" (1 Cor. 14:15, NLT). Music is simply a language, so style is fluid and worship leaders have a responsibility to determine the best musical language for interacting with God. There is nothing wrong with worshiping in a polka style, but my guess is that the polka is not the best musical language with which your church family can worship. Your worship should become and should stay *contemporary* in the very best sense of being the best language for your congregation to converse with God.

So if a church is adding a second or third service anyway to fit in more people, and if there is an opportunity to provide a "corporate voice" that can make worship more intelligible for a distinct segment of the church body, doesn't it make sense to go that route? Perhaps. I've done it. I've been part of efforts to design and create alternate services several times. But if we really cut to the chase, I think it's more God-honoring for multiple services to worship in the same "voice" even when we're worshiping at a different time and in a different room. Doing so demonstrates a commitment to this value of unity and communicates to worshipers that the whole church is speaking as one, even if they are logistically apart.

If, on the other hand, a church offers multiple styles knowing full well that doing so is just accommodating a split in the congregation into different camps, even if it would resolve conflicts regarding worship style, I believe that decision is a rejection of unity that will disappoint God. The best way to *reach people* is to genuinely meet God in worship together, regardless of style, and display the attractiveness of our corporate relationship with God. The unbeliever "will worship God and declare that God is really among you" (1 Cor. 14:25). But how much better for worshipers to learn that worship is not for their pleasure, that worship involves having the attitude of

Christ, and that Jesus desires for us to live, serve and worship *together*, in unity. I, personally, am more interested in making decisions based on the potential of pleasing God rather than pleasing worshipers. If unity is important to Him, which it is, I want to do everything I can to pursue that value.

God wants us to worship in unity, and if we want to please God, our path is clear. We can make every effort to stop dividing ourselves over worship style and to have the selfless attitude of Jesus in deciding to worship side-by-side with our church family. If you personally come to this place of maturity and decide to worship in unity, side-by-side with those unlike you, it probably won't be in your preferred style. That's fine. Worship leaders committed to unity in worship will prayerfully find a style that is the best expression for all of you together— that's their job. But it may not be your personal favorite. As a mature Christian, you need to let it go and engage anyway. In doing so you will please God. Should you hope for a compromise of styles—a little of your style, a little of my style? Nope. What's the expression? "In for a penny, in for a pound," or something like that? If you are choosing unity, don't even worry about getting it a little bit your way. Let it go and engage anyway with the very best attitude possible. In doing so you are pleasing God.

When our son Connor was four, he was listening in as we prayed with some friends. Later in the day he asked me, "Daddy, what were those people doing when you prayed?"

I responded, "What do you mean, Connor?"

He said, "When they made those funny noises."

And then he reproduced for me what he thought he had heard. I figured it out and explained to him that often when people pray together, they agree with each other, and sometimes they express affirmation and agreement with their "noises."

Later that day we sat down for a meal, and I began praying: "Dear Lord (GRUNT! SNORT! BIG GRUNT! from Connor), thank you for your goodness and love (GRUNT!

GRUNT! GRUNT!), and thank you for providing this food (GRUNT! HUGE GRUNT! SNORT!)."

Becky and I almost did our own snorting trying to hold in our laughter. Bless Connor's heart. He was agreeing with me in prayer.

We may not agree about everything when we join together as Christ's bride to worship. We may have different personal preferences. We may have different skin color. We may come from different generations and look at the world differently. We may manage our money differently, we may raise our kids differently, and we may be voting for different presidential candidates. There may even be issues in God's Word that we interpret differently. But we can agree that Jesus Christ is the Son of God. Amen? We can agree that He died and rose again so that we can have eternal life through faith in Him. Amen? We can agree that He is the holy and righteous Lamb of God who is worthy of our praise and adoration. Amen? That makes us His bride, and we can find unity in our worship. We may have to work at it. It may be sacrificial and awkward, but this is how the bride of Christ gathers to love her Groom. It is what Paul had in mind in his prayer for the Romans (Rom. 15:5–6). It is what Jesus Christ had in mind when He prayed that we would "be one, just as you and I are one, Father (John 17:21)."

Questions to Think About

1. Does your church please God by pursuing unity in worship? Do people of all ages worship together at your church? Do the demographics in your worship gatherings reflect the demographics in your community?
2. Have you personally made choices based on your worship style preference rather than selflessly pursuing unity? Are you making those same choices now? Can you choose unity now rather than self?
3. Are you still involved in petty worship style disagreements? If so, how will you ever be ready to judge angels and judge the world (see 1 Cor. 6:1–6)?

8

Pleasing God by Worshiping in Truth

But the hour is coming, and is now here,
when the true worshipers will worship the
Father in spirit and truth, for the Father is
seeking such people to worship him.
John 4:23

We looked earlier at this John 4 passage in which Jesus
has a conversation with the Samaritan woman. We saw
what Jesus was *not* interested in—the *where*, or the form of
worship—in contrast to what the He *was* interested in—
worshipers who worship in spirit and truth. I suggested that
"worshiping in spirit" refers to the ability of our spirits to
connect with God, who is Spirit. It is our capacity of having a
personal relationship with Him. That was the focus of
chapter 5, "Pleasing God by Worshiping with Authenticity." I
also said that the *truth* part had to do with knowing that God's
Word is truth and that Jesus Himself is "the way, the truth, and
the life" (John 14:6). If the Father "is seeking such people to
worship Him" (John 4:23) it is worth more time and attention
to understand what this means for us.

The Truth of God's Word

To worship "in truth" means that our minds must be fully engaged in seeking, finding, understanding, and applying the truth of God's Word. We must worship rightly in response to the person and power of God as revealed to us in Scripture. The Bible carries with it the authority of God, and it is the only infallible rule "to teach us what is true and to make us realize what is wrong in our lives. It straightens us out and teaches us to do what is right" (2 Tim. 3:16, NLT, 1st edition). Jesus said to the Father, "Your word is truth" (John 17:17, NIV), which means that the Bible defines truth and all truth conforms to biblical truth. The Father is seeking those who worship rightly—who worship in full conformity to biblical truth.

This starts with the doctrinal stance of your church regarding the Bible. I trust that your church holds the Bible in the very highest regard and affirms that "all Scripture is breathed out by God" (2 Tim. 3:16) and contains the very Words of God. Conformity to biblical truth then becomes evident in the teaching/pulpit ministry of your church. It is vital that preaching be grounded and centered on God's Word, but the commitment to truth at your church spreads rather quickly into the other elements of worship.

Singing with Understanding

I lead three worship services at my church each Sunday, but to accommodate growth, there are two more worship gatherings that meet in another room that I do not lead. Other teams plan and lead these gatherings. I remember a flurry of emails some months ago having to do with song selection in one of these gatherings. Here's an edited version of the original email. Although it wasn't written to me, I was copied as the Worship Pastor.

I am writing to discuss some of the worship selections for the worship gathering. It is with much prayer and counsel that I write. I pray that humility will characterize this email, and whatever correspondence/discussion results. I feel that some of the worship songs selected on Sundays are not appropriate for congregational singing because they:

1. are theologically incorrect,
2. are singer-focused (rather than God-focused),
3. contain lyrics that are too abstract to understand and relate to, or
4. contain lyrics that are too individualized to understand and relate to.

I have included the lyrics to two songs that have been sung ... recently that I feel contain at least one of these characteristics. (These are the first that come to mind.) I have highlighted in bold the lyrics that I find troubling. I am not commenting on whether these songs are beneficial to listen to on the radio in your car. They very well may be. But I am questioning their appropriateness for congregational worship.[16]

So what do you think about that? We'll get to the two songs later, but first let's look at a few things about this note. First, I know the guy who wrote this email, and I believe that it truly was written in humility and honesty, and that should characterize every conversation between disagreeing Christians. The attitude that is brought to a conflict is usually more powerful than any argument.

Second, it is awesome when there is a theological awareness among worshipers and a desire to express truth in our worship. Several worshipers at my church are quick to bring a lyric or phrase to my attention if they aren't sure how it conforms to the truth of God's Word. My choir recently sang a great anthem that is a setting of the first six verses of Isaiah 35.

I hadn't talked with the choir about the setting, so one of my choir members wanted to know what the song was about— what did the language mean that God is coming to save us with "divine holy fire" and coming with "a vengeance"? It made more sense when we looked at Isaiah together and talked about the biblical context.

I remember other instances as well. One was a discussion with someone about the phrase, "Open the eyes of my heart," from Paul Baloche's song with that title. Does the heart have eyes? This person thought it was a strange concept and had trouble singing those words. I agree with her; it is a strange phrase. But then we looked at the biblical basis for the words. It is lifted from Ephesians 1:18 where Paul uses that imagery, "the eyes of your hearts," to pray for spiritual enlightenment. He is praying for something different than what we ask God for in that particular song, but the phrase itself has a biblical precedent.

As another example, we recently sang the Israel Houghton song, "Friend of God,"[17] and one of our worshipers was troubled by the concept of the almighty God, whom we worship with reverence, also being our friend. The song is based, of course, on Jesus's words in John 15: "You are my friends if you do what I command you. No longer do I call you servants, . . . but I have called you friends" (John 15:14–15). God is both transcendent and immanent, and through Christ, incredibly, we enjoy a new closeness with Him. But I love it when worshipers have this kind of awareness and the willingness to engage with me to ensure that we worship in truth. (May they become just as aware of the other eight values that please God, which we discuss in chapters 4–7 and 9–12.)

As a side note, it's a good idea to avoid tackling topics like this via email. Good communication involves voice inflections, body language, and immediate give-and-take. You get none of that in emails, and innocent comments can inadvertently offend. Get in the same room and talk about it.

This is the kind of stuff that, even if handled rightly and humbly, can feel like a personal attack. It's good to have this kind of discussion, but it can be ticklish, so do it face to face.

Finding Truth in Our Songs

Let's look at a couple of the phrases in the two songs in question for the purpose of discussing truth in our worship. My intent is not to pick on these two songwriters, but I do want to show some of the interaction we had regarding these songs. There were more phrases that were questioned, but it might be helpful as we consider the pursuit of truth in our worship to look at just a few examples. The phrase from the song is followed by the email writer's comments:

"When all of a sudden, I am unaware of these afflictions eclipsed by glory."
What does this mean? Why am I singing it?

"And my heart turns violently inside of my chest."
Why does my heart turn violently? What does this mean? Why am I singing about this?

"I don't have time to maintain these regrets."[18]
What regrets? What does this mean? Why am I singing this?

And the second song has the phrase:

"You make everything glorious."[19]
This isn't theologically correct.

As the emails went back and forth, I eventually participated in the discussion. I am not showing you all of the emails, but I think you'll get the essence of the exchange. Again, we should have talked about this in person; I was guilty as well. Here, though, are some comments I made, referring back to the four points in the first email.

1. *Some of our songs are theologically incorrect.*

Of course our songs need to be rooted in truth. Absolutely. I think if I pick a song, I need to be able to open my Bible and explain or justify every phrase of the song. As a rule of thumb, if I'm uncomfortable trying to explain a song, I probably shouldn't be using it!

2. *Some of our songs are singer-focused (rather than God-focused).*

I agree that our worship should ultimately be God-focused, but I also see that many of the Psalms begin with a singer focus. They use the pronoun *I* and begin with very personal experiences and feelings that lead to a recognition that the answer is *God*—His sovereignty, His power, His love, and so forth. But the authors of the Psalms certainly brought their personal stuff before God. I just opened my Bible at random and glanced at Psalm 13. That is one example out of many.

3. *Some of our songs contain lyrics that are too abstract to understand and relate to.*

Not every song needs to have a deep theological message. This is true in the Psalms as well; some are profound and others quite simple (see Psalm 131). But they still must all express truth.

4. *Some of our songs contain lyrics that are too individualized to understand and relate to.*

I agree that we need to understand what we are singing. I think you could build quite a strong argument from 1 Corinthians 14 that our corporate worship needs to be *intelligible*. This should influence our *style* discussions as well as our *content* discussions. But since songs are poetry, not prose, it isn't necessary for everything to be perfectly literal, nor does a song need to say everything there is to say about a particular truth. Even individual Bible passages don't do that.

I went on in my email to respond to the specific song phrases by saying that some of us are *thinkers* and some of us are *feelers*, and a lot of us are in the middle somewhere. *Feelers* could very well be deeply moved by the first song and find rich meaning in the imagery and the language. This song could express powerfully a personal experience with the grace of Jesus. Very cool. *Thinkers* might not see clarity in the vivid language, the multiple metaphors, and the oblique phrases, while *feelers* might be deeply moved. Being aware of both the thinking and feeling dimensions, how would the average worshiper interact with this song? Some might not pause to consider it, but if pressed, would the average worshiper: (1) know what these phrases mean, and (2) find meaning and application in his or her experience? It is often good to challenge worshipers a little bit, but ultimately, is there enough inherent worth in the song to overcome the issues of clarity and application so that this song is a meaningful corporate expression of God's love and grace intersecting our messed-up lives? Maybe; maybe not.

The second song, which contains the phrase, "You make everything glorious," is challenging as well. The writer of the email asserted that the phrase is not theologically correct, which drives us to Scripture for our answer. Of course we will some day share in Christ's glory and heaven and earth will be made new. But the issue in this song is the use of the present tense: "You *make* everything glorious." Is it true that everything is glorious now? The term *glorious* is a rather high standard. In the Bible it is used mostly in reference to some aspect of God and His glory.

In terms of God's creation, Scripture says that:

1. He made everything good (Gen 1:31).
2. He sustains all creation (Col. 1:17).
3. Everything will someday be made new (Rev. 21:1).
4. But we also know that the ground was cursed (Gen. 3:17), that creation is in "bondage to corruption" (Rom. 8:21), and that the whole creation is currently groaning (Rom. 8:22) under the weight of sin.

In regard to people, however, the Bible says:

1. He made us "good" (Gen. 1:31). We were created in His image (Gen. 1:27).
2. We will someday be raised "in glory" (1 Cor. 15:42–43).
3. We are a "new creation"—all things have become new (2 Cor. 5:17).
4. We are in the process of being sanctified—our minds are being renewed and transformed (Rom. 12:2).
5. We reflect God's glory and "are being transformed into the same image [of the Lord] from one degree of glory to another" (2 Cor. 3:18).
6. But we aren't there yet. We still sin (James 3:2).

So does the song say that I am *now* glorious? Maybe 2 Corinthians 3:18 suggests that I am at a *degree of glory* as I become more like Christ, but I still take exception to the idea that I am now glorious. And is *everything* glorious? It will be, but it is not currently in the way I understand the word in its biblical sense.

I may not have gotten everything right in my contribution to the discussion, but this is an example of how we may need to wrestle with the issue as we seek the goal of committing to the truth of God's Word in our worship. And I reiterate the first thing I said in my email: "As a rule of thumb, if I'm uncomfortable trying to explain a song, I probably shouldn't be using it!" That's true for a worship leader selecting songs, and it's true for a worshiper singing songs.

May our minds be engaged in processing the content of everything that happens in worship. I quoted this verse earlier: "I will pray in the spirit, and I will also pray *in words I understand*. I will sing in the spirit, and I will also sing *in words I understand*" (1 Cor. 14:15, NLT). If you sing without paying attention or without understanding the words coming out of your mouth, you need to recommit to worshiping *in truth*. Your mind needs to fully plug into the conversation. If you are not convinced of the truth of any content, I recommend the following steps:

1. Stop singing that particular song or mouthing that particular response until you have resolved your discomfort.
2. Do your own research. Many, perhaps most of the songs we sing at church are paraphrases or settings of Scripture. Do some digging to understand the origins and the context of the song. You may discover something that makes that song much more meaningful for you.
3. Then, if you are still uncomfortable, humbly and graciously ask the worship leadership to help you understand the song or the phrase.

There is great value in this kind of honest searching for truth in worship.

New versus Old

I want to briefly expand on one of the points I made in my email. There is a somewhat common misconception that traditional stuff often contains more truth and greater doctrinal depth than contemporary stuff and that new songs are more shallow and contain less truth than old songs. This is lazy thinking, because content and style are two separate issues. There is good old stuff and bad old stuff. There is good new stuff and bad new stuff. Some of our most treasured hymns are certainly deep and rich, but so are many new songs by great, new songwriters.

Let me give you some examples. I can't think of any traditional hymn that conveys the profundity of God's sovereignty like *You Are God Alone (Not a god)* by Billy and Cindy Foote with phrases like this: "You are God alone, from before time began. . . . And right now, in the good times and bad, You are on Your throne, You are God alone."[20] Also, consider songs that convey the awesome concepts of biblical passages such as this: "Then Job arose and tore his robe and shaved his head and fell on the ground and worshiped. And he said, 'Naked I came from my mother's womb, and naked shall I return. The LORD gave, and the LORD has taken away; blessed be the name of the LORD'" (Job 1:20–21). I don't know of any hymn that expresses these verses in a way that compares to what Matt and Beth Redman did with the song *Blessed Be Your Name*. "When I'm found in the desert place, though I walk through the wilderness, blessed be Your name."[21] And there are few hymns that convey the sufficiency of Christ like *I Will Glory in My Redeemer*, by Steve and Vicki Cook, or *In Christ Alone*, by Stuart Townend and Keith Getty.[22] And these particular songwriting teams have written many other great, new songs.

Are there shallow new songs? Sure. But there are plenty of older songs in the hymnal that could be criticized as shallow as well. John Frame identifies song controversies in the evangelical awakening of the 1700s as well as the evangelical music in the late-nineteenth century when the music was criticized as "too popular, too subjective, doctrinally imprecise, impoverished, or worse."[23] These are hymns in our hymnbooks. Of course criticizing a song as *shallow* is precarious, as I mentioned in the email, given the thematic simplicity and repetition of some of the Psalms.

New or old isn't the point. Whatever content we include in our worship should contain the truth of God's Word. Sometimes that will be profound and sometimes simple. Sometimes that can start with my experiences and feelings as a child of God and sometimes it can be declarations of God's character. We should, though, derive our content from God's Word, and we should be able to hold our lyrics up to God's Word as our standard and our arbiter of truth.

The Truth of Jesus Christ

The other aspect of worshiping in truth is recognizing Jesus's words when He identifies Himself:

> I am the way, the truth, and the life.
>
> John 14:6

> Then Pilate said to him, "So you are a king?" Jesus answered, "You say that I am a king. For this purpose I was born and for this purpose I have come into the world—to bear witness to the truth. Everyone who is of the truth listens to my voice."
>
> John 18:37

And John speaks powerfully about truth in the person of Christ:

> And the Word became flesh and dwelt among us, and we have seen his glory, glory as of the only Son from the Father, *full of grace and truth*.
>
> John 1:14

Jesus Christ came to reveal God to us, and it is in looking to Jesus that we know God. We find the truth of God in the person of Jesus. For this reason, our worship centers on Jesus.

> For the law was given through Moses; *grace and truth* came through Jesus Christ.
>
> John 1:17

Jesus fulfills Old Testament teaching, and God's faithfulness to His people culminates in Jesus becoming flesh and dwelling among us. Above and beyond the loving kindness God extended to Israel, Jesus becomes the greatest and ultimate expression of grace and truth. All of the elements of Old Testament worship point to Jesus. Once again drawing from John Frame's book, Jesus is the ultimate sacrifice for sin, thus bringing an end to the temple offerings. "Jesus is also the one who *brings* the ultimate sacrifice; that is to say, he is the ultimate priest," and He is the ultimate Mediator. "Jesus is God's dwelling among men. The purpose of the temple was to point forward to Him. ... All the tabernacle and temple furniture speak of Christ." He is "Lord of the Sabbath." He is the focal point of the annual feasts. He is the Passover Lamb. He sends His Spirit, He fulfills the Day of Atonement through His blood, and He embodies the Feast of Tabernacles. He is the true Israel. Frame fleshes out all of these concepts, showing how Christ fulfills the Old Testament, but ultimately Frame says, "Clearly, then, Christian worship should be full of Christ. We come to the Father only by Him (John 14:6). In worship we look to Him as our all-sufficient Lord and Savior. Christ must be inescapably prominent and pervasive in every occasion of Christian worship."[24]

I ask my online class this question: "Some churches observe communion every week, some once a month, and some even more infrequently. If our worship is indeed 'full of Christ,' should we not remember His work at His table every week? Why or why not?" The students respond with good insights regarding the observance of communion, but it also helps them think more broadly. The question is not really about the frequency of communion; it just uses communion as a springboard for considering the question: "Is our worship 'full of Christ?'" What can we do to make our worship more Christ-centered? More frequent communion is one possible way of focusing our worship on Him. Certainly we worship planners can make sure that we always exalt Jesus, relate the gospel, and respond to His sacrificial atonement. Jesus said, "I am the way, and the truth, and the life. No one comes to the Father except through me" (John 14:6). In all of our worship, may we "come to the Father, through Jesus the Son, and give Him the glory, great things He hath done!"[25]

The Father is seeking those who worship in spirit and in truth. May our worship be centered on the truth of God's Word and on the person of Jesus Christ, full of grace and truth, as we try to be those worshipers for whom the Father is looking.

Questions to Think About

1. Do you know what you sang last Sunday morning? Were you aware of what you were singing? Did you understand what you were singing? Did you agree with what you were singing?

2. Are you primarily a *thinker* or a *feeler*? How does this affect the way you worship? If you are a *feeler*, do you need to engage more with your mind? If you are a *thinker*, do you need to uncover your emotions a little more?

3. What do you think about communion? Our worship should be *full of Christ*. Would a weekly observance of communion help us keep His atoning sacrifice as a focal point of our gatherings?

9

Pleasing God by Worshiping in Purity

Who shall ascend the hill of the LORD? And who shall stand in his holy place? He who has clean hands and a pure heart, who does not lift up his soul to what is false and does not swear deceitfully. He will receive blessing from the LORD and righteousness from the God of his salvation.

Psalm 24:3–5

I have some interest in the phenomena of what we often call "revival." At times, God's awesome power has descended on His Church like fire—consuming, purging, and transforming. These can be amazing periods in which souls are saved and lives are transformed in extraordinary ways. In some traditions, churches schedule "revivals" and pursue these unusual manifestations of the Spirit's power. Other traditions, presumably, desire and expect that God will work in their midst continually, and there is little attention given to special revival times. I read a book by Elmer Towns and Douglas Porter in which they recount what they consider to be *The Ten Greatest Revivals Ever.*[26] We will look at three of those top ten revivals.

Great Revivals in History

The *1904 Revival* has been described by J. Edwin Orr as "the most extensive evangelical awakening of all time" and as "a blaze of evening glory at the end of the Great Century."[27] It is estimated that over five million people around the globe accepted Christ during a two-year period. Beginning as a concentrated prayer effort at Moody Bible Institute and the Keswick Convention in England, the revival first manifested itself in two prisoner of war camps in Bermuda and Ceylon and then spread to South Africa, the home of many of the released prisoners. This was followed by the "awakening" in Japan, Australia, and New Zealand and the Welsh Revival that spread quickly onto the European Continent and to North America, India, Korea, Indonesia, Africa, and Latin America. In the U.S., the awakening was manifested in the Azusa Street Revival in California, an occurrence to which several major Pentecostal denominations trace their roots. The influences of this worldwide revival were felt for decades, as evidenced, for instance, by reduced alcoholism and crime in Great Britain and a wave of morality in the United States that resulted in the Eighteenth Amendment to the Constitution, which established Prohibition, and a purge of corrupt politicians throughout the nation. Extensive missionary efforts can be traced to this revival as well.

The origins of the *First Great Awakening* (1727–1750) have been traced to a group of Moravian Christians in Germany meeting to observe the Lord's Supper. The revival that occurred in their community led to a prayer meeting that lasted twenty-four hours a day for a hundred years! The revival spread to England and to the American colonies and embraced the ministries of Jonathon Edwards, George Whitefield, and the Wesley brothers. John Wesley converted the energy of revival into the formation of the Methodist Church. Towns and Porter note that spiritual awakenings can lead to other kinds of awakenings as well. They postulate that the First Great

Awakening in New England was the impetus for change in the political climate that resulted in the American Revolution and the formation of the United States of America.[28]

The *General Awakening* (1830–1840) began in Rochester, New York, with the ministry of Charles Finney and eventually spread to Europe, Africa, Asia, and the Pacific, notably Hawaii. In America alone, it is estimated that 100,000 converts were added to the church in just the first year of the revival. One lasting legacy of the General Awakening was the great Sunday school movement that swept through the Midwest United States, with many of the Sunday schools evolving into Methodist and Baptist churches.

Those were amazing times, but they raise a lot of questions in my mind. Why did God choose to do such amazing things in those particular time spans? Why doesn't He do this all of the time? Does God work in the same way today? Everywhere? Somewhere? Anywhere? Should this be the way He always works? Could it be? If so, why would He? Or even if it is not happening on a global scale, is God demonstrating His power at your church? Are souls being saved and lives being transformed where you worship?

In the U.S., I am not aware of any large-scale revivals in recent years that are comparable to these historic movements in scope or spiritual impact. And it is probably true that many churches are not, in fact, experiencing the power of God's Spirit sweeping through their worship and into the other facets of their ministry in a way that is similar to those great revivals. I hope and pray that God is present and active in your congregation. Maybe He is working, but on a lesser scale and with results that are less dramatic. I am sure that is true in many churches. But many of us are missing out. Church life and worship may seem quite mundane. Why does God sometimes act in very dramatic ways and at other times seem distant? We go through the motions of worship but nothing really *happens*. We sing the songs, say the prayers, and listen to the sermon but nothing *changes*. Perhaps we are really seeking Him. Where then is God? Why is He not drawing near and displaying His power? Where is revival? Why are there churches that aren't growing and aren't seeing anyone new come to saving faith in Christ?

I think there is an answer. Here are some examples we can look at in which God chose to keep His distance from His people.

God Keeping His Distance

The chosen people of Israel wandered often and far from God, as recorded throughout the Old Testament. The Northern Kingdom was finally exiled to Assyria because of their sin:

> And they abandoned all the commandments of the LORD their God, and made for themselves metal images of two calves; and they made an Asherah and worshiped all the host of heaven and served Baal. And they burned their sons and their daughters as offerings and used divination and omens and sold themselves to do evil in the sight of the LORD, provoking him to anger.
>
> 2 Kings 17:16–17

Finally their defiance and rejection of God's laws was so great that "the LORD was very angry with Israel and *removed them out of his sight*" (2 Kings 17:18). It happened in the Southern Kingdom as well. Judah was exiled to Babylon, Zedekiah became king, and "it came to the point in Jerusalem and Judah that *he cast them out from his presence*" (2 Kings 24:20). Isaiah made it clear, "It's your sins that have cut you off from God" (Isa. 59:2, NLT).

David was confronted by the prophet Nathan after his sinful episode with Bathsheba and Uriah. As he lamented and grieved over his sin, he pleaded to God, "Cast me not away from your presence, and take not your Holy Spirit from me" (Ps. 51:11). The New Testament church in Laodicea was not as blatantly sinful, but God still reacted to their "lukewarm" condition: "Would that you were either cold or hot! So, because you are lukewarm, and neither hot nor cold, I will spit you out of my mouth" (Rev. 3:15–16). But in verse 20, Christ is standing outside the door, knocking, and waiting to be invited to enter.

So why does God not draw near and display His power? The answer is *sin*. God keeps His distance where there is sin. David asks in Psalm 24:

> Who shall ascend the hill of the LORD?
> And who shall stand in his holy place?
> *He who has clean hands and a pure heart,*
>   who does not lift up his soul to what is false
>   and does not swear deceitfully.
> He will receive blessing from the LORD
>   and righteousness from the God of his salvation.
>
> Psalm 24:3–5

Paul says to the Romans, "I bring you the Good News so that I might present you as an acceptable offering to God, *made holy by the Holy Spirit*" (Rom. 15:16, NLT). Anything less than holiness is unacceptable to a holy God and will not please Him.

God desires to draw near to us. He desires to pour out His Spirit on us and accomplish great things for His kingdom as we corporately worship Him. The problem is sin. Our sin and hard hearts impede a holy God from drawing close and establishing intimacy with His beloved bride. This is not a matter of forgiveness. When we trust Christ for salvation, Christ's righteousness is imputed to us. We are clean and forgiven through the blood of Christ. We can say with assurance the words of the old gospel song, "My sins are blotted out, I know."[29] So unconfessed sin is not a positional issue, it is a relational issue. It also is not a question of the indwelling of the Holy Spirit. Jesus promised that His

109

followers would have the Holy Spirit, "even the Spirit of truth, whom the world cannot receive, because it neither sees him nor knows him. You know him, for he dwells with you and will be in you" (John 14:17). But it is an issue of emotional distance. As discussed in our chapter about authenticity, we can be close or we can be far from God. If there is sin in our lives, it is repugnant to our holy God, and He will pull away.

Neither my wife nor I are holy. Far from it. Like every married couple, we have experienced the effect of sin in our relationship, and we understand the emotional distance that can result from hurtful words or harmful actions. I am in a secure position with Becky; we love each other deeply, and we are committed to each other "'til death do us part." But we still sometimes encounter an emotional chilliness when a wrong has been committed. We experience distance in our relationship. The antidote is a softening of hearts, confessions of pride, and expressions of repentance that take place before we can begin restoring the emotional intimacy of our relationship.

That's the way it is in many of our churches. There is an emotional chilliness in our corporate relationship with God, and it is the direct result of unconfessed sin. Considering God's holiness and His absolute abhorrence of sin, it is no wonder that He does not draw near and do anything special if there are indeed hard hearts and a lack of repentance in His Church. If we go through the motions and nothing happens, and if we sing the songs, say the prayers, and listen to the sermon but nothing changes, it is because of sin and unrepentant hearts.

Confession of Sin

Here is the common link between the great revivals in history. Those times in which God has drawn near and poured out His power have been initiated by corporate confession, repentance, and brokenness. Towns and Porter note that according to one observer, the 1904 revival was characterized "by extraordinary prayer, by faithful preaching, conviction of sin, confession and repentance." In 1727, those gathering at the Moravian communion service recognized that all was not right among them, and they determined to "quit judging each other." And Charles Finney strongly emphasized accountability before God in his sermons, which lead to the Rochester Revival of 1830 and the General Awakening.[30]

God's desire is for broken and contrite hearts, and He will respond with awesome power when we seek His mercy on our knees. God made a promise to Solomon that was dependent on the humility of the Israelites. The familiar words of 2 Chronicles 7:14 state: "If my people who are called by my name will humble themselves, and pray and seek my face and turn from their wicked ways, I will hear from heaven and will forgive their sins and heal their land." God promised to respond if the Israelites did those four things: (1) humble themselves, (2) pray, (3) seek God's face, and (4) turn from their wicked ways. I think we can apply that promise to ourselves; doing those four things pleases God. We quoted David earlier as he dealt with his sin with Bathsheba. Later on in the chapter he declares: "You do not desire a sacrifice, or I would offer one. You do not want a burnt offering. The sacrifice *you desire* is a broken spirit. You will not reject a broken and repentant heart, O God" (Ps. 51:16–17, NLT).

Am I saying that if your church is stuck it is because of sin rather than methodology? Maybe so. Am I saying you are stuck because of sin rather than a lack of a dynamic teaching ministry, wonderful worship, or great youth ministry or because of a dying congregation, a bad location, an aging facility, or whatever else? Maybe so. Is there a toxic environment among the people and the leaders of your church? It's all about sin. I am claiming the promises of Scripture that if we draw near to God, He will draw near to us. I am saying that if God observes broken and repentant hearts in your congregation, He will be delighted, He will draw near, and He will display His power, and the toxicity will be transformed

111

into unity. I am saying that if your church truly, truly humbles themselves, prays, seeks God's face, and turns from sin, your "stuck" church could spark a revival and witness an incredible outpouring of God's Spirit. Is it "them" at church who are the problem? As I always tell my kids, "You're not responsible for 'them.'" Trust God to work on them. *You* take care of *you* . . . and pray.

I admit that as a Worship Leader, I do not always do a good job of leading my congregation in repentance and confession. It is a crucial first step toward experiencing God's mighty presence, but it is a tough first step. Confession is not a popular activity. It is not encouraging, uplifting, or celebratory in nature to ask people to consider their sin—but it is vital. It was a necessary part of Isaiah's interaction with God. He saw God's glory and responded, "Woe is me! For I am lost; for I am a man of unclean lips, and I dwell in the midst of a people of unclean lips; for my eyes have seen the King, the LORD of hosts!" (Isa. 6:5). Moses had a similar response when he met God in the burning bush and "covered his face" (Exod. 3:6, NLT). Likewise, when John encountered Jesus, he says, "I fell at His feet as if I were dead" (Rev. 1:17). Then God used all three of these men in mighty ways. Only when we are humbled and truly repentant will God use us in mighty ways.

My son Connor used to have a beanbag in his room that looked like a big football. When Connor was five, Becky asked him one day to pick up the toys in his room. He was upstairs for a while, and when he came downstairs Becky asked him if his room was cleaned. Connor gave an affirmative response. Becky, however, knowing her son very well, followed up with a second question.

"Connor, if I went upstairs and looked in your room would I be happy?"

Connor took some time considering both the question and his response, and finally asked her a question in return: "Would you be looking under my football pillow?"

112

Is there sin tucked away in your life somewhere about which you haven't come clean with God? If you've let it go long enough, your conscience has probably become seared. You have rationalized the sin and convinced yourself that it isn't so bad. Compared to other sins or other people, you're looking pretty good. How about comparing it to God's holiness? May we fall at His feet, like John, and see our sin. Before worshiping we should check under our football pillows to ensure that everything is cleaned up in our rooms. We should pause, reflect, and consider whether there are impediments in our relationship with God. If we soften our hearts and come with spirits of repentance, God will draw intimately near and perhaps release His power.

Questions to Think About

1. Have you witnessed revival or seen God do an extraordinary work in a specific time and place? Can you explain why?
2. Are souls being saved and lives being transformed at your church right now? Why or why not?
3. Is there anything going on in your life that is wrong? Is there anything that you are rationalizing or choosing to push away from your consciousness—hiding it under the "football pillow"? Will you confess it now and receive God's forgiveness and cleansing? "If we confess our sins, he is faithful and just to forgive us our sins and to cleanse us from all unrighteousness" (1 John 1:9).

113

10

Pleasing God by Worshiping Sacrificially

I appeal to you therefore, brothers, by the mercies of God,
to present your bodies as a living sacrifice, holy and acceptable
to God, which is your spiritual worship.
Romans 12:1

A re there sermons you have heard that stick in your memory? I have a few. I remember coming back to my home church after being away at college and hearing the new pastor preach on Hebrews 10. It was great. I still remember parts of that sermon some thirty years later.

Old Testament Sacrifices vs. New Testament Sacrifices

The pastor explained that for all the attention given to the sacrificial system in the Old Testament, "It is impossible for the blood of bulls and goats to take away sins" (Heb. 10:4). That's why the priests' work was never over. They had to keep at it every day, and it was never enough. "And every priest stands daily at his service, offering repeatedly the same sacrifices, which can never take away sins" (Heb. 10:11). Our pastor painted a vivid picture of the daily effort and perhaps drudgery of sacrificing bulls and goats—over and over and over. The blood, the stench, and the mess.

But then the chapter gets to the work of Jesus Christ:

> But when Christ had offered for all time a single sacrifice for sins, he sat down at the right hand of God, waiting from that time until his enemies should be made a footstool for his feet. *For by a single offering he has perfected for all time those who are being sanctified.*
>
> Hebrews 10:12–14

When Christ offered Himself, He was the perfect sacrifice. Chapter 9 of Hebrews explains a little more:

> Thus it was necessary for the copies of the heavenly things to be purified with these rites, but the heavenly things themselves with better sacrifices than these. For Christ has entered, not into holy places made with hands, which are copies of the true things, but into heaven itself, now to appear in the presence of God on our behalf. Nor was it to offer himself repeatedly, as the high priest enters the holy places every year with blood not his own, for then he would have had to suffer repeatedly since the foundation of the world. But as it is, he has appeared once for all at the end of the ages to put away sin by the sacrifice of himself.
>
> Hebrews 9:23–26

Christ offered Himself "once for all" to "put away sin." His sacrifice was fully sufficient for the atonement of sin.

When his sermon reached the verse in Hebrews 10 in which Christ "sat down at the right hand of God," our pastor sat down. He walked over to a chair, plopped down into it, crossed his legs, and spread his arm over the next chair. It was over. The work was done. The final sacrifice was enough. No more sacrifices, no more bulls, no more goats, no more blood. I clearly remember him slouching down on that chair to illustrate the completion of Christ's work. May Jesus Christ be praised for His sacrifice and for the redemption of our sins through His blood. And just as I pointed out the phrase "pleasing aroma," as we looked at acceptable sacrifices in the Law, so we notice the fragrance of Christ's sacrifice, "As Christ loved us and gave himself up for us, a *fragrant offering and sacrifice* to God" (Eph. 5:2).

So the Old Testament rituals are over, and yet we are still challenged by some New Testament language. Peter writes, "You yourselves like living stones are being built up as a spiritual house, to be a holy priesthood, *to offer spiritual sacrifices* acceptable to God through Jesus Christ" (1 Peter 2:5). What's that about? If the sacrificial system is over, why are we being called to offer sacrifices? And what are "spiritual sacrifices"? Are those different than Old Testament sacrifices? Here are some passages that shed some light on what a "spiritual sacrifice" is:

1. *Financial gifts.*

"I have received full payment, and more. I am well supplied, having received from Epaphroditus the gifts you sent, a fragrant offering, *a sacrifice acceptable and pleasing to God*" (Phil. 4:18).

In this instance, financial gifts are a sacrifice that is "acceptable and pleasing to God." Have you considered that putting money in the offering plate could be part of achieving our goal in worship—that of pleasing Him? We get hung up on the offering because we've seen the greed and manipulations of preachers on TV. Some churches put baskets in the back because they don't want to offend people by passing a plate. But we have to get over that and understand the significance of giving our money as an act of worship.

2. *Praise.*

"Through him then let us continually offer up *a sacrifice of praise* to God, that is, the fruit of lips that acknowledge his name" (Heb. 13:15).

In this case, the offering of praise is shown to be a sacrificial offering that we bring. We bring "psalms and hymns and spiritual songs, singing and making melody to the Lord" (Eph. 5:19). We'll come back to that shortly, because there's more to be said about our praise.

3. *Service and generosity.*

"Do not neglect to do good and to share what you have, for such *sacrifices are pleasing to God*" (Heb. 13:16).

Are you involved in providing food for the homeless? Do you put away the sound equipment after the worship service or work in the nursery? Do you care for orphans or visit those in prison? Acts of service and generosity toward others are sacrificial offerings that we bring for the pleasure of God.

4. *Your whole life.*

"I appeal to you therefore, brothers, by the mercies of God, to present your bodies as *a living sacrifice*, holy and acceptable to God, which is your spiritual worship" (Rom. 12:1).

Beyond the giving of gifts, beyond the praise of our lips, beyond acts of service, we offer our whole lives as living sacrifices. This is our ultimate spiritual sacrifice. We give to God every thought, every word, and every action. We are fully His—body and soul. We come as living sacrifices.

These passages show a sacrificial *attitude* that extends beyond the Old Testament rituals. Sprinkling blood on the altar is obsolete, but worshiping with a giving, sacrificial, self-denying heart will bring delight to God and will be a fragrant aroma—acceptable and pleasing to Him. Romans 15:5 states that we can find harmony together and worship together only when we each have the attitude of Christ Jesus toward the each other. The attitude of Jesus was one of humility and sacrifice—ultimately sacrificing His own life. So when we adopt that same attitude, we come humbly, looking out for the interests of others (see Phil. 2:2–4), yielding our own preferences, and willing to sacrifice all.

Expending Effort in Worship

Even in the Old Testament, God makes it clear he cares more about a sacrificial attitude than He does about the sacrifice itself (see Prov. 21:3; Isa. 1:11, 16–17; Hosea 6:6; Amos 5:22–24; Micah 6:6–8). And David understood that. Do you remember the episode in 2 Samuel 24 when David counted the fighting men of Israel? David had sinful motives when he took a census of the military, and when he faced Gad, the prophet, he was given a choice of punishments:

> "Thus says the LORD, Three things I offer you. Choose one of them, that I may do it to you." So Gad came to David and told him, and said to him, "Shall three years of famine come to you in your land? Or will you flee three months before your foes while they pursue you? Or shall there be three days' pestilence in your land? Now consider, and decide what answer I shall return to him who sent me." Then David said to Gad, "I am in great distress. Let us fall into the hand of the LORD, for his mercy is great; but let me not fall into the hand of man."
>
> 2 Samuel 24:12–14

So David chose three days of a severe plague throughout the land at the hand of the Lord. Then God mercifully cut short the three days just as the angel of death was preparing to destroy Jerusalem. At Gad's prompting, David obediently went to the threshing floor of Araunah the Jebusite, where the angel of death had stopped, in order to offer burnt offerings to make things right with God. Araunah and David had this exchange:

> "Let my lord the king take and offer up what seems good to him. Here are the oxen for the burnt offering and the threshing sledges and the yokes of the oxen for the wood. All this, O king, Araunah gives to the king." And Araunah said to the king, "May the LORD your God accept you." But the king said to Araunah, "No, but I will buy it from you for a price. *I will not offer burnt offerings to the LORD my God that cost me nothing.*"
>
> 2 Samuel 24: 22–24

David proceeded to pay for the threshing floor and the oxen and offered his sacrifices, knowing that the offerings themselves had limited value; the real value was in the *personal cost.*

We should come to worship to please God with our sacrificial attitudes—ready to give, to look out for the interests of others, to yield our own preferences, and to offer our whole selves as spiritual sacrifices. This may still seem a little nebulous in terms of practical application. I want to try to rephrase it a little so we can understand what it means for this coming Sunday morning.

We each have a "love language." Have you read those books? I've figured out over the years that there are expressions of love that are very meaningful to Becky and there are other expressions of love that don't really communicate well with her. For instance chocolates, jewelry, and flowers are traditional gifts for wives, but in our case these are less meaningful kinds of gifts. They represent just a token effort—especially if obtained at the last minute. I've learned that there are much better ways of telling Becky I love her on special occasions.

What Becky really appreciates is a gift that requires some *effort* on my part. Running out at the last minute to grab something is not so good. Spending time, thought, and creative effort is very good. Money isn't the issue, instead it is how much of *me* is invested in the gift. I tried writing a poem once. It was awful, but it was the kind of effort that spoke love to Becky. She appreciated that I had spent the time and stepped out of my comfort zone for her. I could bore you with some of my other attempts—some successful, others not so much—but the important ingredient in telling my wife that I love her is my personal *effort*. Am I investing time, thought, creativity, and some exertion in my desire to love her and please her?

I think this is how we think when we come to worship. We come "to offer spiritual sacrifices acceptable to God through Jesus Christ" (1 Peter 2:5). We can think about these sacrifices as expending *effort*. That's what David meant when he talked about a sacrifice that should *cost* something. Here are some suggestions as to how we might expend effort in our worship:

- Spending time in the Word and in prayer each day of the week so that our relationship with God is authentic takes effort. *It is a spiritual sacrifice acceptable to God.*
- Committing to show up at corporate worship, at the expense of other choices in our busy life takes effort. *It is a spiritual sacrifice acceptable to God.*
- Showing up early and eager for worship might take a lot of effort. *It is a spiritual sacrifice acceptable to God.*
- Spending time in personal confession prior to worship takes effort. *It is a spiritual sacrifice acceptable to God.*
- Praying for the time of corporate worship in

advance—that God would draw near and work through the power of His Spirit—takes effort. *It is a spiritual sacrifice acceptable to God.*

- Joining in the singing with our whole self—spiritually, mentally, emotionally, and physically, no matter how well we sing takes effort. *It is a spiritual sacrifice acceptable to God.*

- Joining in the singing even if we don't like the song, the instruments, the key, the volume, or the worship leader takes effort. *It is a spiritual sacrifice acceptable to God.*

- Giving thanks for everything in every circumstance. *This is a spiritual sacrifice acceptable to God.*

- Willingly learning a new song; joining in as soon as we can and as best we can takes effort. *It is a spiritual sacrifice acceptable to God.*

- Not being distracted by lighting, sound, misspelled words, or quirky worship leadership takes effort. *It is a spiritual sacrifice acceptable to God.*

- Not being distracted by a million stray thoughts takes effort. *It is a spiritual sacrifice acceptable to God.*

- Not being offended by anything a fellow worshiper does takes effort. *It is a spiritual sacrifice acceptable to God.*

- Humbling ourselves before the King of kings and Lord of lords takes effort. *It is a spiritual sacrifice acceptable to God.*

- Focusing intently so that we truly understand and mean all that comes from our mouth takes effort. *It is a spiritual sacrifice acceptable to God.*

- Going outside our comfort zone to kneel, to share, to sing, to greet, to stand, or to raise hands can take effort. *It is a spiritual sacrifice acceptable to God.*
- Humbly bringing our needs and weaknesses before the throne of grace in prayer can take effort. *It is a spiritual sacrifice acceptable to God.*
- Giving financially, generously, and selflessly takes effort. *It is a spiritual sacrifice acceptable to God.*
- Interacting with and caring for our fellow worshipers can take effort. *It is a spiritual sacrifice acceptable to God.*
- Asking forgiveness for wronging a brother or sister takes effort. *It is a spiritual sacrifice acceptable to God.*
- Not being critical of the leaders or fellow worshipers but praying for them instead can take a lot of effort. *It is a spiritual sacrifice acceptable to God.*
- Taking notes so that we are listening closely for God's voice takes effort. *It is a spiritual sacrifice acceptable to God.*
- Responding in obedience to God's Word takes effort. *It is a spiritual sacrifice acceptable to God.*

Do you see where we are going with this? The list could be much longer. It turns out that pleasing God in worship is not easy; it requires hard work. It takes much effort. It involves sacrifice. Just as this kind of effort means so much to my wife, Becky, so is it pleasing to our God. This is worship that costs us something.

I have a story about *effort*. When my daughter Caroline was six, she met me at the door one day with a little book she had made, entitled "Daddy—You Are Great When . . ."

Daddy-
You are
great when ...

Each page had a picture illustrating why I was a great Daddy:

Page 1: I'm a great Daddy because I gave her piggy-back rides.

Page 2: I'm a great Daddy because I filled up her pool with water.

124

Page 3: I'm a great Daddy because I helped her rollerblade and ride her bike.

Page 4: I'm a great Daddy because I took her on the water slides at the water park.

Page 5: I'm a great Daddy because I made her pancakes.

Page 6: I'm a great Daddy because I played checkers with her.

Page 7: I have no idea! We can't remember! Those things are brown, but that still doesn't help us remember. But whatever they are, I am a great dad because of them!

I've always treasured Caroline's book. Eleven years later I am still talking about it, and it's still tucked away in a drawer in my desk (along with numerous expressions of love from her creative little sister Callie). It is an expression of her love for me that touches my heart every time I revisit the pages. But it obviously is not the level of *excellence* that impresses me and convinces me of her love. It is the *effort* Caroline expended that communicates her love for me—the effort it took to think through our relationship and articulate her feelings through her pictures.

We don't pick an unblemished goat out of the herd and sacrifice it on an altar to cover our sins anymore. Jesus's sacrifice made that obsolete. His blood has been shed. But we can still please God by offering worship that is *costly*. By offering worship that requires *effort*. By offering worship that sacrificially yields our comforts and our desires for the sake of others and for God's sake. This is worship that pleases God.

Excellence in Worship

Just a quick word about *excellence*. I just said that it wasn't the level of excellence that spoke to me in Caroline's book, but it was the effort she made. This may sound to some like a "dumbing down" of worship. I know that most worship ministries strive for excellence. Worship leaders and worshipers are looking for and expecting a high degree of excellence in the planning and execution of the worship service. And yet if *effort* is the key to expressing love, then does it even matter if the outcome is any good? I think excellence does matter, but in our pursuit of excellence we may be missing the point and perhaps causing harm.

I view excellence in worship as the summation of three biblically based ingredients: aptitude, empowerment, and effort.

1. *Aptitude.* We all have God-given gifts (1 Corinthians 12), and we are to identify our gifts and use them in ministry. God has wired each of us to do certain things well, and fulfillment and purpose come in finding our unique niche for ministry. There are people who as part of Christ's body have a natural, God-given capacity to communicate through some sort of creative expression, and generally speaking, it is those people who belong in worship leadership.

2. *Empowerment.* The role of a pastor is to equip these people for service (see Eph. 4:12)—to nurture relationships with them, mentor them, train

them, give them tools and resources, encourage them, and set them free to use their gifts.

3. *Effort*. We've already been discussing this third ingredient. Effort involves preparation, prayer, hard work, and more (see Col. 3:23).

When these three ingredients are combined, they *result* in excellence.

I am not convinced that there is an objective level of excellence that, if reached, has great inherent value to God. In fact, people get run over and hurt when excellence is the endgame. I am convinced, though, that if we give the right people the right tools, and that if we all bring our best effort, this process does have great value to God. And we will "play skillfully on the strings, with loud shouts" (Ps. 33:3) as Scripture calls us to do. The resulting worship will be excellent.

Questions to Think About

1. Do you expect to *get* in worship, or do you expect to *give*. Do you expect to receive, or do you expect to offer? In what ways was your worship *costly* last Sunday morning?
2. In what ways can you determine to expend more effort this coming Sunday morning so that you are bringing acceptable sacrifices to worship? Did anything on the list on pages 121-123 catch your attention as an area in which you can worship more sacrificially?
3. Have you been part of worship that is not excellent or is even sloppy? Do you think it was an issue of aptitude, equipping, effort, or something else? Conversely, have you been aware of hurt feelings at church because someone was not "good enough" to assist in the leading of worship? How does this all fit in with "worshiping with sacrifice"?

11

Pleasing God with the Fruit of Our Lips

Oh come, let us sing to the LORD; let us make a joyful noise
to the rock of our salvation! Let us come into his presence
with thanksgiving; let us make a joyful noise to him
with songs of praise!
Psalm 95:1–2

Make a joyful noise to the LORD, all the earth!
Serve the LORD with gladness! Come into his presence
with singing! Know that the LORD, he is God! It is he who
made us, and we are his; we are his people, and the sheep of his
pasture. Enter his gates with thanksgiving, and his courts
with praise! Give thanks to him; bless his name!
For the LORD is good; his steadfast love endures forever,
and his faithfulness to all generations.
Psalm 100

The concepts of *praise* and *thanksgiving* are often where we
start when we think about worship. We've glossed over
them a little bit to this point. Not because they aren't crucial
components of our worship; they are. Others have written
entire studies focusing just on our expressions of praise and
thanksgiving, and deservedly so. But we've waited until now

so that we can understand praise and thanksgiving in the broader context of all that goes on in a worship conversation. In a sense, our praise and thanks emanate out of the other eight values of gathering, authenticity, engagement, unity, truth, purity, sacrifice, and action. Here's some context for understanding the significance of our *praise* and *thanksgiving*.

The Fruit of Our Lips

The author of the book of Hebrews says, "Through him then let us continually offer up a sacrifice of praise to God, that is, the *fruit of lips* that acknowledge his name" (Heb. 13:15). The term *fruit of lips* suggests that what comes out of our mouth is the produce or outgrowth of what is inside. Fruit is *produced* by healthy trees and healthy vines. For us, that health comes as we abide in Jesus and walk in the Spirit. Jesus said, "I am the vine; you are the branches. Whoever abides in me and I in him, he it is that bears much fruit, for apart from me you can do nothing" (John 15:5). Paul prays for the Colossians, noting that as they grow in their understanding of the knowledge of God, they will walk worthy of the Lord and will bear fruit:

> And so, from the day we heard, we have not ceased to pray for you, asking that you may be filled with the knowledge of his will in all spiritual wisdom and understanding, so as to walk in a manner worthy of the Lord, fully pleasing to him, *bearing fruit* in every good work and increasing in the knowledge of God.
>
> Colossians 1:9–10

As we grow in Christ, one of the results is the fruit of our lips. "What you say flows from what is in your heart" (Luke 6:45, NLT). Our praise doesn't spring from nothing. It is an outgrowth of our spiritual eyes opening and our ever-increasing awareness of the wonder of God.

Similarly, our thanksgiving is *fruit*. It is a result of having lives built on Christ and establishing roots that "grow down into Him."

> And now, just as you accepted Christ Jesus as your Lord, you must continue to follow him. Let your roots grow down into him, and let your lives be built on him. Then your faith will grow strong in the truth you were taught, *and you will overflow with thankfulness.*
>
> Colossians 2:6–7, NLT

Paul's familiar words in Colossians 3 link singing and thanksgiving with two elements of growth—letting "the Word of Christ dwell in you richly" and interacting with other believers "in all wisdom":

> And let the peace of Christ rule in your hearts, to which indeed you were called in one body. And be thankful. *Let the word of Christ dwell in you richly, teaching and admonishing one another in all wisdom,* singing psalms and hymns and spiritual songs, *with thankfulness in your hearts to God.* And whatever you do, in word or deed, do everything in the name of the Lord Jesus, giving thanks to God the Father through him.
>
> Colossians 3:15–17

Again in Ephesians, praise and thanksgiving goes hand in hand with being "filled with the Spirit"—another indicator of our inner spiritual condition.

> And do not get drunk with wine, for that is debauchery, *but be filled with the Spirit,* addressing one another in psalms and hymns and spiritual songs, singing and making melody to the Lord with your heart, *giving thanks always* and for everything to God the Father in the name of our Lord Jesus Christ.
>
> Ephesians 5:18–20

FOR WHOSE PLEASURE?

We don't start worship with praise and thanksgiving. We start by knowing God. Then as we see His greatness and glory, our response is to humbly praise Him. As we increasingly understand His awesome works, our expressions of thanksgiving naturally flow from our lips in response. Our praise and thanks become the fruit of a healthy and vibrant relationship with God.

Sacrificial Praise

A second point about our praise and thanks is that they are a spiritual sacrifice (which we discussed in the previous chapter). Hebrews 13:15 refers to our "sacrifice of praise." Asaph says, "Make thankfulness your sacrifice to God. . . . Giving thanks is a sacrifice that truly honors [God]" (Ps. 50:14, 23, NLT). David says, "I will praise the name of God with a song; I will magnify him with thanksgiving. This will please the LORD more than an ox or a bull with horns and hoofs" (Ps. 69:30–31). Our praises and our thanks are sacrificial because of what we give up. In offering our praise, we give up our pride. We recognize the almighty character of God and the supremacy of Jesus Christ and come humbly, putting ourselves in a position of submission at His feet. We lower ourselves and lift Him up. In offering our thanks, we give up our sense of entitlement. Thanksgiving is an antidote to the self-absorption we looked at in chapter 2. In giving thanks, we join Job and Paul in living lives of gratitude in the midst of any circumstances. We don't grasp, but with our eyes on the eternal, we are grateful for every spiritual blessing.

Created to Praise

Our ultimate purpose as Christ's bride is to proclaim His praise and glorify Him. And when it is the fruit of an authentic relationship with God and when it is a sacrificial offering, our praise and thanksgiving bring pleasure to God. God said He had formed the nation of Israel "that they might declare my praise" (Isa. 43:21). He told Jeremiah that He would "give them one heart and one purpose: *to worship me forever*" (Jer. 32:39, NLT). Peter includes the Gentiles in God's holy nation—His Church—and gives them the same purpose: "But you are a chosen race, a royal priesthood, a holy nation, a people for his own possession, *that you may proclaim the excellencies of him* who called you out of darkness into his marvelous light" (1 Peter 2:9). Perhaps these were some of the verses that guided the crafters of the Westminster Shorter Catechism, which states that "man's chief end is to glorify God, and to enjoy him forever." And we know that eventually "every knee will bend to me, and every tongue will confess and give praise to God" (Rom. 14:11, NLT).

As evidence of His pleasure, we see times in the Bible in which God responds to praise and thanks by blessing His people with His presence and His power. David said to God, "You are holy, enthroned on the praises of Israel" (Ps. 22:3). Then there is the awesome story in 2 Chronicles of the dedication of the temple:

> And when the priests came out of the Holy Place (for all the priests who were present had consecrated themselves, without regard to their divisions, and all the Levitical singers, Asaph, Heman, and Jeduthun, their sons and kinsmen, arrayed in fine linen, with cymbals, harps, and lyres, stood east of the altar with 120 priests who were trumpeters; and it was the duty of the trumpeters and singers to make themselves heard in unison in praise and thanksgiving to the LORD), and when the song was raised, with trumpets and cymbals and other musical instruments, in praise to the LORD, "For he is good, for his steadfast love endures forever," the house, *the house of the LORD, was filled with a cloud, so that the priests could not stand to minister because of the cloud, for the glory of the LORD filled the house of God.*
> 2 Chronicles 5:11–14

God showed His pleasure with the praise of His people by visiting them in a dramatic way.

Similarly, another story in 2 Chronicles shows God responding to the praise of His people with a demonstration of His power. There's more to the story, but we'll just pick it up in the middle:

> Then Jehoshaphat bowed his head with his face to the ground, and all Judah and the inhabitants of Jerusalem fell down before the LORD, worshiping the LORD. And the Levites, of the Kohathites and the Korahites, stood up to praise the LORD, the God of Israel, with a very loud voice.
>
> And they rose early in the morning and went out into the wilderness of Tekoa. And when they went out, Jehoshaphat stood and said, "Hear me, Judah and inhabitants of Jerusalem! Believe in the LORD your God, and you will be established; believe his prophets, and you will succeed." And when he had taken counsel with the people, he appointed those who were to sing to the LORD and praise him in holy attire, as they went before the army, and say, "Give thanks to the LORD, for his steadfast love endures forever."
>
> *And when they began to sing and praise, the LORD set an ambush against the men of Ammon, Moab, and Mount Seir, who had come against Judah, so that they were routed.*
>
> 2 Chronicles 20:18–22

In this case, God blessed His people with a dramatic display of His power and might on their behalf. In doing so, He showed His delight in their praise.

As we read these stories, we gain some perspective. We should see the silliness of pursuing our own agenda in corporate worship gatherings. How shortsighted to think of ourselves when we are encountering the almighty King, the Creator of the universe, the great I AM. It is only His response that matters. May God find delight in our worship as we aim to please Him and as we offer our spiritual sacrifices. May He be honored through our dependence on Him and our expressions of gratitude. May He be glorified in our humility and our songs of praise. May the fruit of our lips be acceptable in His sight.

Questions to Think About

1. Only one sits on the throne. In genuine praise, we exalt Him and lower ourselves. What is your *position* in worship? Are you humbly bowing at His feet, or are you lifting yourself to a place of importance?
2. Do you give thanks always? Do you recognize God's providential hand in every circumstance, or do you feel that life is unfair? How can your thinking change so that gratitude constantly flows from your lips as fruit from your heart?
3. You have been chosen to "proclaim the excellencies of Him who called you out of darkness into His marvelous light" (1 Peter 2:9). This is your calling. Is there more you can do to proclaim His excellencies?

12

Pleasing God and Worship in Action

Do not neglect to do good and to share what you
have, for such sacrifices are pleasing to God.
Hebrews 13:16

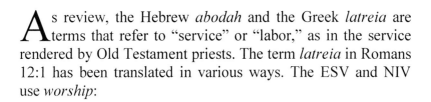

As review, the Hebrew *abodah* and the Greek *latreia* are
terms that refer to "service" or "labor," as in the service
rendered by Old Testament priests. The term *latreia* in Romans
12:1 has been translated in various ways. The ESV and NIV
use *worship*:

> "Present your bodies as a living sacrifice, holy
> and acceptable to God, which is your spiritual
> *worship*" (ESV).

> "Offer your bodies as a living sacrifice, holy
> and pleasing to God—this is your true and proper
> *worship*" (NIV).

The King James translates the word as "service":

> "Present your bodies a living sacrifice, holy,
> acceptable unto God, which is your reasonable
> *service*" (KJV).

The NASB doesn't want to choose, so they use both:

> "Present your bodies a living and holy sacrifice, acceptable to God, which is your spiritual *service of worship*" (NASB).

Whichever way the term is translated, there is a connection between *worship* and *service*. There is a linkage between *worship* and the *work of worship*. In the Old Testaments, the *work of worship* involved the duties that the priests diligently labored at accomplishing. Since Christ, it is the work we do in offering ourselves as living sacrifices. This work of *presenting our bodies* is the ultimate summation of our response in worship. Our minds, our hearts, our physical bodies, and our wills are all encapsulated in the supreme offering of our bodies as living sacrifices.

We have been looking at pleasing God primarily in the context of preparing for corporate worship and then engaging in our worship gatherings. But worship does not stop when the service is over. This final value, *worship in action*, will take a further look at what it means to "present our bodies" and what it means to tackle the work of worship as we leave the gathering and live individual lives of worship.

Worship in Action in Scripture

We've noted that biblical worship encounters include a call to action. In Isaiah's case, he saw God's glory and responded with confession and an awareness of his sinfulness. God responded by granting forgiveness and Isaiah received cleansing. Then God called him to action or service:

> I heard the voice of the Lord saying, "Whom shall I send, and who will go for us?" Then I said, "Here am I! Send me." And he said, "Go, and say to this people:

'Keep on hearing, but do not understand; keep
on seeing, but do not perceive.' Make the heart of this
people dull,
   and their ears heavy,
   and blind their eyes;
lest they see with their eyes,
   and hear with their ears,
   and understand with their hearts,
   and turn and be healed."

Isaiah 6:8–10

Moses was called to action when he encountered God in the burning bush (see Exodus 3). As a result of this meeting with God, he rescued the Israelites from Pharaoh's slavery, delivered the Ten Commandments, and led God's people to the edge of the Promised Land. The apostle John encountered Jesus in his vision (see Revelation 1). He was commissioned to record his vision, providing us with insight into God's plan for the ages. Saul encountered God on the road to Damascus. His name was changed to Paul, and he traveled around his world preaching Christ and eventually penned letters to the churches that we know as the Pauline Epistles. Peter and John knew Jesus, saw Him glorified at His transfiguration, received the Holy Spirit at Pentecost, and through His power preached and performed signs and wonders that jump-started the early church. As a result of meeting God, these men were called to action.

In one sense, service is part of a broad definition of worship, as mentioned in chapter 4. Service is an element of living lives of worship—glorifying God with every word and deed. Worship *includes* lives of service as we respond to His call and say, "Here am I, send me." A second way to view this is that our service is an inevitable *result* of our worship. If we view corporate worship as a more specific interaction with God—the Groom meeting His bride—then service will always *follow* worship. In a sense, it is a test of our worship. I think both views are correct. But either way, if we just come to church and go home and are not involved in service, we

139

haven't worshiped. We have flunked Worship 101. God-pleasing worship will always include a call or a challenge to respond to God's Word and an affirmative response from the worshiper. If we meet God like Isaiah, Moses, John, or Saul/Paul did, we will answer with a "Yes! Put me in, coach! Tell me where to go and how to serve!"

Following is a visual representation to help show this relationship between a worship encounter and the service that naturally flows out of it.

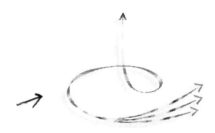

Many of the aspects of corporate worship are represented in these swirly arrows by the upward motion. We have gathered as His bride, communicated our love, aggressively sought Him, and known His nearness. In His presence we have experienced His love and been renewed and transformed. So far the movement has been up, toward Him. But the movement doesn't stop at the top; the arrows also flow in the other direction—back down and out. Peter, James, and John may have wanted to erect tents and linger in glory at Christ's transfiguration, but there was work to do.

There is also a cycle that continually recurs as we come to worship and then turn around and leave. As we are changed and energized from meeting God, we disperse and return to the world, as did Paul, Moses, and the others, to serve Christ and live for Him.

Worship in Action—Hearts of Obedience

Many churchgoers do indeed flunk this test of service. It is possible to hear a call from God's Word and to respond by saying "no." Have you heard the stats? I don't remember the numbers, but it's something like only 20 or 30 percent of attendees who do all the work at church.

Callie is our third (and youngest) child. When she was two, her mom asked her to do something. Not only did she say "no," but out of the mouth of a two-year-old came the words, spoken with energy and vehemence: "NO . . . FOREVER!" And then she slammed the door to her room in Becky's face! Do you believe that? And it's a better story when you can hear Becky imitate her tone of voice. Pure defiance!

Unbelievably, that's how worshipers sometimes respond. They hear God's instructions, but they don't *do* anything or make any changes. That is defiance. Here are the words of God, spoken through His prophets:

> This is what the LORD of Heaven's Armies, the God of Israel, says: "Take your burnt offerings and your other sacrifices and eat them yourselves! When I led your ancestors out of Egypt, it was not burnt offerings and sacrifices I wanted from them. This is what I told them: '*Obey me*, and I will be your God, and you will be my people. *Do everything as I say*, and all will be well!'"
>
> Jeremiah 7:21–23, NLT

> Has the LORD as great delight in burnt offerings and sacrifices, as in obeying the voice of the LORD? Behold, *to obey* is better than sacrifice, *and to listen* than the fat of rams.
>
> 1 Samuel 15:22

God says that our worship has no value to Him if we go through the motions but are unwilling to obey. Can we worship, go sleep with a partner outside of marriage, and please God? No. Can we worship, walk out the door and fight with our parents, and please God? No. Can we worship, go look at pornography, and please God? No. Can we worship, cheat our employer, and please God? No. Can we worship, ignore a world in need of food, shelter, and the Savior, and please God? No. If our heart is not in a position of obedience, then our worship cannot please God. Don't even bother trying.

Worship in Action through the Power of God's Spirit

We can't obey by ourselves. "For if you live according to the flesh you will die, but if by the Spirit you put to death the deeds of the body, you will live" (Rom. 8:13). Obedience and true ministry only happen as we are empowered by God's Spirit. Peter was a wimp before Pentecost. Moses was cowering in the desert before he encountered the burning bush. We are incapable of bringing glory to the Father through our lives without His power infusing us. Do you remember Ezekiel and his vision of the dry bones? Consider his story:

> The LORD took hold of me, and I was carried away by the Spirit of the LORD to a valley filled with bones. He led me around among the old, dry bones that covered the valley floor. They were scattered everywhere across the ground. Then he asked me, "Son of man, can these bones become living people again?"
>
> "O Sovereign LORD," I replied, "you alone know the answer to that."
>
> Then he said to me, "Speak to these bones and say, 'Dry bones, listen to the word of the LORD! This is what the Sovereign LORD says: Look! I am going to breathe into you and make you live again! I will put flesh and muscles on you and cover you with skin. I will put breath into you, and you will come to life. Then you will know that I am the LORD.'"

So I spoke these words, just as he told me. Suddenly as I spoke, there was a rattling noise all across the valley. The bones of each body came together and attached themselves as they had been before. Then as I watched, muscles and flesh formed over the bones. Then skin formed to cover their bodies, but they still had no breath in them.

Then he said to me, "Speak to the winds and say: 'This is what the Sovereign LORD says: Come, O breath, from the four winds! Breathe into these dead bodies so that they may live again.'"

So I spoke as he commanded me, and the wind entered the bodies, and they began to breathe. They all came to life and stood up on their feet—a great army of them.

Ezekiel 37:1–10, NLT, 1st edition

As Ezekiel watched, a vast pile of old, dry bones were reconnected to each other, took on muscles and flesh, and were covered with skin. They rattled around a bit, but the bodies had no life. Then, as instructed, Ezekiel prayed for the Spirit of God to breathe life into the bones, and the wind entered the dead bodies and brought them to life. And they arose and became a great army.

In worship, God's people can encounter His person, humble themselves, and become infused with the Spirit's power. Then God does His molding, melding, filling, and using. Without the breath of God's Spirit on us we are but rattling bones without life. All of the ministries we have at our churches may have muscles and flesh and bones—they may look good—but without an infusion of God's power, they are lifeless and will ultimately accomplish little. Without God's Spirit we are wimps like Peter (Matt. 26:69–75) and cower in hiding like Moses (Exod. 2:14–15). The effectiveness of all the ministries of the church hinge on God's Spirit being breathed into God's people. And it is in worship that God's Spirit breathes life into our corporate dry bones and we come alive and become a mighty army.

Worship in Action

So we come to worship with a willingness to obey, we invite and allow the Holy Spirit to breathe on us, and then finally, we are ready for action.

> To *do righteousness and justice* is more acceptable to the LORD than sacrifice.
>
> Proverbs 21:3

> What to me is the multitude of your sacrifices? says the LORD;
> I have had enough of burnt offerings of rams and the fat of well-fed beasts;
> I do not delight in the blood of bulls, or of lambs, or of goats. . . .
> Wash yourselves; make yourselves clean; remove the evil of your deeds from before my eyes; cease to do evil, *learn to do good; seek justice, correct oppression; bring justice to the fatherless, plead the widow's cause.*
>
> Isaiah 1:11, 16–17

> I want you to *show love*, not offer sacrifices. I want you *to know me* more than I want burnt offerings.
>
> Hosea 6:6, NLT

> But *let justice roll down like waters, and righteousness like an ever-flowing stream.*
>
> Amos 5:24

> He has told you, O man, what is good; and what does the LORD require of you but to *do justice, and to love kindness, and to walk humbly with your God?*
>
> Micah 6:8

144

In the Old Testament, the sacrificial system was crucial, but it was still just the outward manifestation of hearts seeking to obey and serve God. If God's people truly loved Him, they would not only be faithful at the temple, but they would kick into action and live lives seeking justice, correcting oppression, bringing justice to the fatherless, and pleading the widow's cause. And then in the New Testament we read:

> But I will rejoice even if I lose my life, pouring it out like a liquid offering to God, just like your *faithful service* is an offering to God.
>
> Philippians 2:17, NLT

> Don't forget to *do good and to share what you have with those in need*. These are the sacrifices that please God.
>
> Hebrews 13:16, NLT

Doing good and sharing with those in need are acts of obedience—part of the action in our worship that is pleasing to God. In fact, if we back up a little bit in Hebrews, we are exhorted to "offer to God acceptable worship, with reverence and awe, for our God is a consuming fire" (Heb. 12:28–29). Then our Bibles show a chapter break. But it could be that the author of Hebrews rolled right into our chapter 13, listing examples of the *acceptable worship*:

> Let brotherly love continue. Do not neglect to *show hospitality* to strangers, for thereby some have entertained angels unawares. *Remember those who are in prison*, as though in prison with them, and those who are mistreated, since you also are in the body. *Let marriage be held in honor among all*, and *let the marriage bed be undefiled*, for God will judge the sexually immoral and adulterous. *Keep your life free from love of money, and be content with what you have*.
>
> Hebrews 13:1–5

This is the action of worship: To go and please Him through serving. To seek justice, correct oppression, bring

145

justice to the fatherless, and plead the widow's cause. To let justice roll down like waters, and righteousness like an ever-flowing stream. To do justice, love kindness, and walk humbly with our God. To do good and share what we have with those in need. To produce fruit (John 15:8), let our light shine (Matt. 5:16), struggle through life together (Gal.6:2), and make disciples (Matt. 28:19). To show hospitality and remember those in prison. To hold marriage in honor and to be content with what we have (Heb. 13:1–5) All of these things and more.

Worship doesn't end with the benediction. Instead, worshipers who please God will listen in obedience, be filled with His Spirit, and then be released into action, arising to become a mighty army.

Questions to Think About

1. Does your church resemble a valley of dry, rattling bones making a lot of noise, or is it like a mighty army? Why?
2. Do you know your gifts? If so, what are they?
3. Service is a test of our worship. Are you consistently using your gifts in ministry? Are you part of the minority doing the work of the church, or are you part of the majority who are not responding to God's call to service in worship? List the ways you are serving.

13

Pleasing God and Finding Joy

My soul will be satisfied as with fat and rich food,
and my mouth will praise you with joyful lips.
Psalm 63:5

Let's review the nine biblical values we have discussed. These are in a different order because there isn't really any particular order.

- Pleasing God involves having an _authentic relationship_ with Him first, so that coming to worship with others allows for even greater intimacy. If our hearts are far away, our worship is a farce. *1*
- Pleasing God involves having a _heart that is clean._ "If we confess our sins, he is faithful and just to forgive us our sins and to cleanse us from all unrighteousness" (1 John 1:9). When we come humbly and with repentant hearts, He promises to draw near and bless— possibly in a mighty way. *2*
- Pleasing God involves gathering as Christ's bride and rejoicing in our Groom _together._ God delights in His gathered people. *3*
- Pleasing God involves finding _unity_ in our *4*

worship. God desires for us to be one just as the Father and Son are one. He will take delight when we deny ourselves and choose to worship with those like and unlike us.

5 • Pleasing God involves *engaging* in worship—being an active participant with our hearts, minds, souls, and bodies rather than being critical spectators.

• Pleasing God involves worshiping in the *truth* of God's Word and in the person of Jesus Christ, for we find the truth of God in Jesus. The Father is seeking those who will worship "in spirit and in truth."

6 • Pleasing God involves worshiping with a *sacrificial attitude*—ready to give, to look out for the interests of others, to yield our own preferences, and to offer our whole selves as spiritual sacrifices. We can also understand this as expending *effort* in worship.

• Pleasing God involves offering the *fruit of our lips*—praise and thanksgiving that demonstrate humble and grateful hearts.

7 • And pleasing God involves *serving*. It is an inevitable result of genuine worship. When we meet God, we are filled with the power of His Spirit and become a mighty army.

There are many tough choices encapsulated in these nine values. There is hard, demanding work involved in pleasing God. These principles require sacrifice, humility, brokenness, effort, service, and a general denial of self.

This shouldn't be surprising. "The sacrifices of God are a broken spirit; a broken and contrite heart, O God, you will not despise" (Ps. 51:17). Getting a right relationship with God means first getting the right *position* before God. That position is one of humility and selflessness. He is the Potter and we are the clay. He is the Creator and we are the created. Every knee will eventually bow before Him. The sooner we learn to humbly bow and acknowledge His reign in our lives, the sooner we will get that position right, and then we will experience His grace and learn to please Him. But living humbly before Him can be tough. Jesus said, "If anyone would come after me, let him deny himself and take up his cross daily and follow me" (Luke 9:23). It couldn't be clearer—following Jesus is hard.

Again, we've been duped into thinking otherwise. The reality is, we aren't the center of the universe, we don't really have any *rights*, there's really no reason we should expect to be *happy*, and nobody really owes us anything. And picking ourselves up by our bootstraps doesn't really guarantee us anything either. There! Is that blunt enough? Turn off the TV and put down the book if you are hearing the worldly message that *it's all about you*. It's not! Reread Philippians 2:1–11 and the example of Jesus when He became human. That is the selfless example we are to follow in life and in our worship.

Joy in Worship

But there is an ironic twist in God's Word. Even as we humbly bow, broken and contrite, and even as we take up our cross, the Word of God is filled with proclamations of JOY! How does that work? You know the verses well; here is a small sampling:

> You make known to me the path of life;
>   in your presence there is *fullness of joy*;
>   at your right hand are pleasures forevermore.
>   Psalm 16:11

> But may all who seek you *rejoice* and be glad in you.
>   Psalm 40:16

Then I will go to the altar of God,
to God my exceeding joy,
and I will praise you with the lyre,
O God, my God.

Psalm 43:4

Clap your hands, all peoples! Shout to God
with loud songs of *joy*!

Psalm 47:1

My soul will be satisfied as with fat and rich
food, and my mouth will praise you with
joyful lips.

Psalm 63:5

But the righteous shall be glad;
they shall exult before God;
they shall be *jubilant with joy*!

Psalm 68:3

My soul longs, yes, faints
for the courts of the LORD;
my heart and flesh *sing for joy*
to the living God.

Psalm 84:2

Oh come, let us sing to the LORD;
let us make a *joyful noise* to the rock of
our salvation!

Psalm 95:1

But the fruit of the Spirit is love, *joy*, peace,
patience, kindness, goodness, faithfulness.

Galatians 5:22

Though you have not seen him, you love him.
Though you do not now see him, you
believe in him and *rejoice with joy that is
inexpressible* and filled with glory.

1 Peter 1:8

I've got one more Connor story. He is a teenager now and almost as tall as me! Some day he'll catch or surpass me. But this is another story from when he was a little kid.

When he was six years old, Connor's toe got caught in a closing door. It got scrunched pretty good and swelled up and turned all kinds of colors. He was miserable. I remember that Becky and I did everything we could to help and comfort him. I also remember that his two sisters were unusually sympathetic. Go figure. They joined in the efforts of trying to console their brother—bringing him pillows to prop up his foot, ice, a cool drink, blankets, whatever they could think of that might make him more comfortable and ease the pain. We all pampered him.

Things settled down a little bit, and one of us eventually asked, "Connor, how are you feeling now?"

Connor thought about it and responded with one of the most profound utterances ever heard at our house. This goes down in the annals of Klingbeil profundity—although those are short annals. This is what the little guy said:

"My heart feels better but my toe still hurts."

How great is that?

Can we be broken and humble and experience joy at the same time? Yes. In fact Paul said the same sort of thing as Connor. ("Our hearts ache, but we always have joy")(2 Cor. 6:10, NLT). Pleasing God in worship involves a denial of self, but pleasing Him in worship *results* in a profound, significant, and lasting *joy*. It seems contradictory, but we bow, and we are lifted up into His presence. We give, and He showers us with blessings. We sacrifice ourselves, and He recreates us into His image. If we aim to please Him, He will respond by fulfilling the needs of our heart. "Delight yourself in the LORD, and he will give you the desires of your heart" (Ps. 37:4).

Our pursuit of self-gratification is nearsighted. Getting what we want doesn't result in lasting fulfillment. Ask any of the young superstar actresses whose lives have fallen apart

151

even as they are able to get everything they want. Ask any of the sports superstars whose paychecks have allowed them to pursue everything and anything they desire and who then find themselves with shattered lives and broken relationships. Ask the lottery winners who find themselves miserable and bankrupt a short time later. It's no different at church. If we don't get what we want, we can be critical, divisive, and miserable. If we *do* get what we want, we've still been critical and divisive and now are spoiled and still miserable. Getting our church to do things our way won't satisfy us. The pursuit of self is an empty pursuit, and there is nothing at the end of that road. It's a highway to nowhere. Kicking at the wrong goal is a pointless, meaningless exercise, and it's just plain dumb.

But the pursuit of God's pleasure results in joy—and a deeper, more complete joy than we could ever imagine. It's not the fleeting joy that we associate with good things happening. It's a state of our souls that is impervious to our lot in life and the day-to-day struggles of a Christian. It's a joy rooted in God, not in ourselves. Ethan, the Ezrahite said, "Happy are those who hear the joyful call to worship, for they will walk in the light of your presence, LORD. They rejoice all day long in your wonderful reputation. They exult in your righteousness" (Ps. 89:15–16, NLT).

And it's a joy that can't be touched by circumstances. In fact, it's a joy that causes us to rejoice in even bad circumstances (James 1:2) because we have some understanding of God's plans and purposes and can see beyond the immediate. Consider Paul's lot in life:

> Five times I received at the hands of the Jews the forty lashes less one. Three times I was beaten with rods. Once I was stoned. Three times I was shipwrecked; a night and a day I was adrift at sea; on frequent journeys, in danger from rivers, danger from robbers, danger from my own people, danger from Gentiles, danger in the city, danger in the wilderness,

danger at sea, danger from false brothers; in toil and hardship, through many a sleepless night, in hunger and thirst, often without food, in cold and exposure. And, apart from other things, there is the daily pressure on me of my anxiety for all the churches.

2 Corinthians 11:24–28

Yikes! And you thought you had it bad! And Paul told the Philippians, "Even if I am to be poured out as a drink offering upon the sacrificial offering of your faith, *I am glad and rejoice with you all*" (Phil. 2:17). And in that joy is the contentment and fulfillment that we all long for. David, even as he was being hunted by his own son, could say, "You *satisfy me* more than the richest feast. I will praise you with songs of joy" (Ps. 63:5, NLT).

So give it up. Give up the pursuit of self gratification when you come to worship. Don't expect to be *pleased*. Quit picking and choosing, criticizing and whining, scrutinizing, and grading. Quit liking or not liking. Quit preferring or not preferring. Quit drinking spiritual milk and start eating solid food in worship. Quit aiming for the wrong goal. Instead, focus on pleasing God. Gather with your church family, be real, be engaged, be united, worship in truth, be pure, be sacrificial, sing His praises, offer your thanksgiving, and go out and serve. *God will be pleased*. He will respond with delight and pour out His grace, His love, His power, and His joy. "Oh what a foretaste of glory divine!"

Questions to Think About

1. Are you at the place of full submission in your relationship with God? Are you bowed at His feet, acknowledging His reign in every aspect of your life? Are you content with whatever circumstance He brings your way—like Joseph, Daniel, and Paul?

2. Are you ready to grow up in your worship? Are you ready to get off the spiritual milk and eat some solid food? Are

you willing to deny yourself? Are you ready for the hard work of worship?

3. Have you experienced the joy that illogically fills the heart of the true worshiper?

Appendix

Pleasing God in Scripture

If you do well, will you not be *accepted*? And if you do not do well, sin is crouching at the door. Its desire is for you, but you must rule over it.

Genesis 4:7

And when the LORD smelled the *pleasing aroma*, the LORD said in his heart, "I will never again curse the ground because of man, for the intention of man's heart is evil from his youth. Neither will I ever again strike down every living creature as I have done.

Genesis 8:21

It shall be on Aaron's forehead, and Aaron shall bear any guilt from the holy things that the people of Israel consecrate as their holy gifts. It shall regularly be on his forehead, that they may be *accepted* before the LORD.

Exodus 28:38

Burn the whole ram on the altar. It is a burnt offering to the LORD. It is a *pleasing aroma*, a food offering to the LORD.

Exodus 29:18

(The phrase "pleasing aroma" is used at least 37 more times in the ESV.)

If his offering is a burnt offering from the herd, he shall offer a male without blemish. He shall bring it to the entrance of the tent of meeting, that he may be *accepted* before the LORD.

Leviticus 1:3

When you offer a sacrifice of peace offerings to the LORD, you shall offer it so that you may be *accepted*.

Leviticus 19:5

And when anyone offers a sacrifice of peace offerings to the LORD to fulfill a vow or as a freewill offering from the herd or from the flock, to be *accepted* it must be perfect; there shall be no blemish in it.

Leviticus 22:21

When an ox or sheep or goat is born, it shall remain seven days with its mother, and from the eighth day on it shall be *acceptable* as a food offering to the LORD.

Leviticus 22:27

And when you sacrifice a sacrifice of thanksgiving to the LORD, you shall sacrifice it so that you may be *accepted*.

Leviticus 22:29

And now, Israel, what does the LORD your God *require* of you, but to fear the LORD your God, to walk in all his ways, to love him, to serve the LORD your God with all your heart and with all your soul.

Deuteronomy 10:12

And Samuel said, "Has the LORD as *great delight* in burnt offerings and sacrifices, as in obeying the voice of the LORD? Behold, to obey is better than sacrifice, and to listen than the fat of rams."

1 Samuel 15:22

I know, my God, that you test the heart and have *pleasure* in uprightness. In the uprightness of my heart I have freely offered all these things, and now I have seen your people, who are present here, offering freely and joyously to you.

1 Chronicles 29:17

. . . that they may offer *pleasing sacrifices* to the God of heaven and pray for the life of the king and his sons.

Ezra 6:10

Let the words of my mouth and the meditation of my heart be *acceptable* in your sight, O LORD, my rock and my redeemer.

Psalm 19:14

May he remember all your offerings and *regard with favor* your burnt sacrifices!

Psalm 20:3

In sacrifice and offering you have *not delighted*, but you have given me an open ear. Burnt offering and sin offering you have not required.

Psalm 40:6

I will not *accept* a bull from your house or goats from your folds.

Psalm 50:9

For you will *not delight* in sacrifice, or I would give it; you will *not be pleased* with a burnt offering.

Psalm 51:16

Then will *you delight* in right sacrifices, in burnt offerings and whole burnt offerings; then bulls will be offered on your altar.

Psalm 51:19

This will *please* the LORD more than an ox or a bull with horns and hoofs.

Psalm 69:31

May my meditation *be pleasing* to him, for I rejoice in the LORD.

Psalm 104:34

Accept my freewill offerings of praise, O LORD, and teach me
your rules.

Psalm 119:108

His delight is not in the strength of the horse, nor his pleasure
in the legs of a man, but the LORD *takes pleasure* in those who
fear him, in those who hope in his steadfast love.

Psalm 147:10–11

Lying lips are an abomination to the LORD, but those who act
faithfully are *his delight*.

Proverbs 12:22

The sacrifice of the wicked is an abomination to the LORD, but
the prayer of the upright is *acceptable* to him.

Proverbs 15:8

To do righteousness and justice is *more acceptable* to the LORD
than sacrifice.

Proverbs 21:3

What to me is the multitude of your sacrifices? says the LORD;
I have had enough of burnt offerings of rams and the fat of
well-fed beasts; I do *not delight* in the blood of bulls, or of
lambs, or of goats.

Isaiah 1:11

For thus says the LORD: "To the eunuchs who keep my
Sabbaths, who choose the things that *please* me and hold fast
my covenant. . . . I will give them an everlasting name that
shall not be cut off."

Isaiah 56:4–5

These I will bring to my holy mountain, and make them joyful
in my house of prayer; their burnt offerings and their sacrifices
will be *accepted* on my altar; for my house shall be called a
house of prayer for all peoples.

Isaiah 56:7

Is such the fast that I choose, a day for a person to humble himself? Is it to bow down his head like a reed, and to spread sackcloth and ashes under him? Will you call this a fast, and a day *acceptable* to the LORD?

Isaiah 58:5

All the flocks of Kedar shall be gathered to you; the rams of Nebaioth shall minister to you; they shall come up with *acceptance* on my altar, and I will beautify my beautiful house.

Isaiah 60:7

What use to me is frankincense that comes from Sheba, or sweet cane from a distant land? Your burnt offerings are *not acceptable*, nor your sacrifices *pleasing* to me.

Jeremiah 6:20

But let him who boasts boast in this, that he understands and knows me, that I am the LORD who practices steadfast love, justice, and righteousness in the earth. For in these things *I delight*, declares the LORD.

Jeremiah 9:24

Though they fast, I will not hear their cry, and though they offer burnt offering and grain offering, I will not *accept* them. But I will consume them by the sword, by famine, and by pestilence.

Jeremiah 14:12

For on my holy mountain, the mountain height of Israel, declares the Lord GOD, there all the house of Israel, all of them, shall serve me in the land. There I will *accept* them, and there I will *require* your contributions and the choicest of your gifts, with all your sacred offerings. As a *pleasing aroma* I will *accept* you, when I bring you out from the peoples and gather you out of the countries where you have been scattered. And I will manifest my holiness among you in the sight of the nations.

Ezekiel 20:40–41

159

And when they have completed these days, then from the eighth day onward the priests shall offer on the altar your burnt offerings and your peace offerings, and I will *accept* you, declares the Lord GOD.

Ezekiel 43:27

As for my sacrificial offerings, they sacrifice meat and eat it, but the LORD does *not accept* them. Now he will remember their iniquity and punish their sins; they shall return to Egypt.

Hosea 8:13

They shall not pour drink offerings of wine to the LORD, and their sacrifices shall not *please* him. It shall be like mourners' bread to them; all who eat of it shall be defiled; for their bread shall be for their hunger only; it shall not come to the house of the LORD.

Hosea 9:4

I hate, I despise your feasts, and I take *no delight* in your solemn assemblies. Even though you offer me your burnt offerings and grain offerings, I will not *accept* them; and the peace offerings of your fattened animals, I will not look upon them.

Amos 5:21–22

Will the LORD be *pleased* with thousands of rams, with ten thousands of rivers of oil? Shall I give my firstborn for my transgression, the fruit of my body for the sin of my soul?" He has told you, O man, what is good; and what does the LORD *require* of you but to do justice, and to love kindness, and to walk humbly with your God?

Micah 6:7–8

Go up to the hills and bring wood and build the house, that I may *take pleasure* in it and that I may be glorified, says the LORD.

Haggai 1:8

Oh that there were one among you who would shut the doors, that you might not kindle fire on my altar in vain! I have *no pleasure* in you, says the LORD of hosts, and I will *not accept* an offering from your hand.

Malachi 1:10

But you say, "What a weariness this is," and you snort at it, says the LORD of hosts. You bring what has been taken by violence or is lame or sick, and this you bring as your offering! Shall I *accept* that from your hand? says the LORD.

Malachi 1:13

You cover the LORD's altar with tears, with weeping and groaning because he no longer *regards* the offering or *accepts* it with favor from your hand.

Malachi 2:13

Then the offering of Judah and Jerusalem will *be pleasing* to the LORD as in the days of old and as in former years.

Malachi 3:4

But in every nation anyone who fears him and does what is right *is acceptable* to him.

Acts 10:35

Those who are in the flesh cannot *please* God.

Romans 8:8

I appeal to you therefore, brothers, by the mercies of God, to present your bodies as a living sacrifice, holy and *acceptable* to God, which is your spiritual worship. Do not be conformed to this world, but be transformed by the renewal of your mind, that by testing you may discern what is the will of God, what is good and *acceptable* and perfect.

Romans 12:1–2

Whoever thus serves Christ is *acceptable* to God and approved by men.

Romans 14:18

. . . to be a minister of Christ Jesus to the Gentiles in the priestly service of the gospel of God, so that the offering of the Gentiles may be *acceptable*, sanctified by the Holy Spirit.

Romans 15:16

So whether we are at home or away, we make it our aim to *please* him.

2 Corinthians 5:9

For am I now seeking the *approval* of man, or of God?

Galatians 1:10

And try to discern what is *pleasing* to the Lord.

Ephesians 5:10

For it is God who works in you, both to will and to work *for his good pleasure*.

Philippians 2:13

I have received full payment, and more. I am well supplied, having received from Epaphroditus the gifts you sent, a fragrant offering, a sacrifice *acceptable and pleasing* to God.

Philippians 4:18

. . . so as to walk in a manner worthy of the Lord, *fully pleasing* to him, bearing fruit in every good work and increasing in the knowledge of God.

Colossians 1:10

But just as we have been approved by God to be entrusted with the gospel, so we speak, not to please man, but to *please* God who tests our hearts.

1 Thessalonians 2:4

Finally, then, brothers, we ask and urge you in the Lord Jesus, that as you received from us how you ought to walk and *to please God*, just as you are doing, that you do so more and more.

1 Thessalonians 4:1

This is good, and it is *pleasing* in the sight of God our Savior.

1 Timothy 2:3

But if a widow has children or grandchildren, let them first learn to show godliness to their own household and to make some return to their parents, for this *is pleasing* in the sight of God.

1 Timothy 5:4

In burnt offerings and sin offerings you have taken *no pleasure*.

Hebrews 10:6

When he said above, "You have *neither desired nor taken pleasure* in sacrifices and offerings and burnt offerings and sin offerings" (these are offered according to the law).

Hebrews 10:8

By faith Abel offered to God a *more acceptable* sacrifice than Cain, through which he was commended as righteous, God commending him by *accepting* his gifts. And through his faith, though he died, he still speaks.

Hebrews 11:4

And without faith it is impossible to *please* him, for whoever would draw near to God must believe that he exists and that he rewards those who seek him.

Hebrews 11:6

Therefore let us be grateful for receiving a kingdom that cannot be shaken, and thus let us offer to God *acceptable worship*, with reverence and awe.

Hebrews 12:28

Do not neglect to do good and to share what you have, for such sacrifices are *pleasing to God*.

Hebrews 13:16

May the God of peace . . . equip you with everything good that you may do his will, working in us that which is *pleasing* in his sight, through Jesus Christ, to whom be glory forever and ever. Amen.

Hebrews 13:20–21

You yourselves like living stones are being built up as a spiritual house, to be a holy priesthood, to offer spiritual sacrifices *acceptable* to God through Jesus Christ.

1 Peter 2:5

And whatever we ask we receive from him, because we keep his commandments and do what *pleases* him.

1 John 3:22

[1] A. W. Tozer, *Worship: The Missing Jewel of the Evangelical Church*, a series of three sermons (Camp Hill, PA: Christian Publications, 1992), 12, 24.

[2] Jean M. Twenge and W. Keith Campbell, *The Narcissism Epidemic* (New York: Free Press, 2009), 60, 69.

[3] Ibid., x.

[4] Ibid, 247–248.

[5] John M. Frame, *Worship in Spirit and Truth: A Refreshing Study of the Principles and Practice of Biblical Worship* (Phillipsburg, New Jersey: P and R Publishing, 1996), 1.

[6] Casting Crowns, "Lifesong" (Reunion, 2005).

[7] Harold M. Best, *Unceasing Worship: Biblical Perspectives on Worship and the Arts* (Downers Grove, Illinois: InterVarsity Press, 2003).

[8] Louie Giglio, *The Air I Breathe: Worship as a Way of Life* (Colorado Springs, Colorado: Multnomah Books, 2003).

[9] Paul E. Billheimer, *Destined for the Throne*, rev. ed. (Minneapolis, Minnesota: Bethany House, 1996), 22–23.

[10] Steve Green, "Antiphonal Praise" (Birdwing Music, 1990).

[11] Laurie Klein, "I Love You, Lord" (House of Mercy Music, 1978).

[12] Søren Kierkegaard, *Purity of Heart Is to Will One Thing* (New York: Harper Torchbooks, 1938), 179–181.

[13] For example, see Psalms 47:1; 63:4; 95:6.

[14] Sally Morgenthaler, *Worship Evangelism: Inviting Unbelievers into the Presence of God* (Grand Rapids, Michigan: Zondervan, 1995).

[15] Frame, *Worship in Spirit and Truth*, 117.

[16] From an email copied to the author, November 19, 2009. Used with permission.

[17] Michael Gungor and Israel Houghton, "Friend of God" (Vertical Worship Songs and Integrity's Praise! Music/Champions for Christ Publishing and Sound of the New Breed, 2003).

[18] John Mark McMillan, "How He Loves" (Integrity's Hosanna! Music, 2005).

[19] David Crowder, "Everything Glorious" (worshiptogether.com songs/sixsteps Music, 2006).

[20] Billy Foote and Cindy Foote, "You Are God Alone (not a god)" (Billy Foote Music, 2004).

[21] Matt and Beth Redman, "Blessed Be Your Name" (Thankyou Music, 2002).

22 Steve and Vikki Cook, "I Will Glory in My Redeemer" (Sovereign Grace Worship, 2001); Stuart Townend and Keith Getty, "In Christ Alone (My Hope Is Found)" (Thankyou Music, 2002).

23 Frame, *Worship in Spirit and Truth*, 116.

24 Ibid., 27–28, 29.

25 "To God Be the Glory," by Fanny J. Crosby, 1875.

26 Elmer Towns and Douglas Porter, *The Ten Greatest Revivals Ever* (Ann Arbor, Michigan: Servant Publications, 2000).

27 J. Edwin Orr, *The Flaming Tongue: The Impact of 20th Century Revivals* (Chicago: Moody Press, 1973).

28 Towns and Porter, *Ten Greatest Revivals*, 72.

29 "My Sins Are Blotted Out, I Know," by Merrill Dunlop, 1927.

30 Towns and Porter, *Ten Greatest Revivals*, 24, 57, 100.

CPSIA information can be obtained at www.ICGtesting.com
Printed in the USA
LVOW101147081011

249685LV00001B/4/P